early years
wishing well

Collected rhymes, stories, songs and information text

# Clothes and food

**Author**
Gill Walton

**Editor**
Clare Miller

**Designer**
Martin Ford

**Compilers**
Stories, rhymes and
information text compiled
by Jackie Andrews

Songs compiled by Peter Morrell

**Assistant Editor**
Saveria Mezzana

**Series Designer**
Anna Oliwa

**Illustrations**
Julie Clough

**Cover artwork**
Alex Ayliffe

Acknowledgements:
Qualifications and Curriculum Authority for the use of extracts from the
QCA/DfEE document *Curriculum guidance for the foundation stage*
© 2000 Qualifications and Curriculum Authority.

The publishers gratefully acknowledge permission to reproduce the following
copyright material:

**Jackie Andrews** for 'The washing machine' and 'A dress for a special day' © 2001, Jackie Andrews, both previously unpublished; **Clive Barnwell** for 'A great big pair of wellington boots' © 2001, Clive Barnwell, previously unpublished; **Ann Bryant** for 'What we wear in my family' and 'What do you like to eat?' © 2001, Ann Bryant, both previously unpublished; **Susan Eames** for 'Getting dressed', 'Jelly', and 'Breakfast's on the table' © 2001, Susan Eames, all previously unpublished; **Val Jeans-Jakobsson** for 'Boots and shoes', 'This is the hat' and 'Fruit' © 2001, Val Jeans-Jakobsson, all previously unpublished; **Karen King** for 'Evie's uniform' and 'The best vegetable' © 2001, Karen King, both previously unpublished; **Patricia Leighton** for 'The sun-hat', 'Mr Bobby's sweet stall', 'Go bananas!' and 'Fish fingers' © 2001,

Patricia Leighton, all previously unpublished; **Johanne Levy** for 'Put on your shirt' © 2001, Johanne Levy, previously unpublished; **Wes Magee** for 'Odd socks in the morning' and 'Dressing up' © 2001, Wes Magee, both previously unpublished; **Tony Mitton** for 'Delicious dishes' © 2001, Tony Mitton, previously unpublished; **Barbara Moore** for 'Auntie Parminder's wedding' and 'Food, glorious food!' © 2001, Barbara Moore, both previously unpublished; **Peter Morrell** for 'Tell us what you're wearing today' © 2001, Peter Morrell, previously unpublished; **Judith Nicholls** for 'Inside out' © 2001, Judith Nicholls, previously unpublished, and for 'Lunch box' from *Higgledy Humbug* by Judith Nicholls © 1990, Judith Nicholls (1990, Mary Glasgow Publications); **Sue Nicholls** for 'Fasteners', 'Picnic surprises!', 'What's

outside the food?' and 'Pop it on a pizza!' © 2001, Sue Nicholls, all previously unpublished; **Jan Pollard** for 'Food for the barbecue' © 2001, Jan Pollard, previously unpublished; **Margaret Willetts** for 'Great Grandma's washing day' © 2001, Margaret Willetts, previously unpublished; **Brenda Williams** for 'Coats', 'Family food sense', 'Cups and saucers' and 'Sam's birthday party © 2001, Brenda Williams, all previously unpublished.

Every effort has been made to trace copyright holders and the publishers apologize for any inadvertent omissions.

Text © 2001 Gill Walton
© 2001 Scholastic Ltd

Designed using Adobe Pagemaker

Published by Scholastic Ltd, Villiers House,
Clarendon Avenue, Leamington Spa, Warwickshire CV32 5PR
Printed by Ebenezer Baylis & Son Ltd, Worcester
Visit our website at www.scholastic.co.uk

1 2 3 4 5 6 7 8 9 0   1 2 3 4 5 6 7 8 9 0

# Contents

Early years wishing well: **Clothes and food**

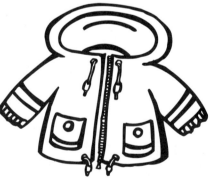

## Wishing Well: Clothes and food

The *Wishing Well* series is designed to help support practitioners working with three- to five-year-olds, during the Foundation Stage of their education. This book is designed to work towards the requirements of the Early Learning Goals. It contains a collection of rhymes, stories, songs and information texts linked to the theme of 'Clothes' and 'Food'.

The activities that accompany these texts are designed to help the children through the stepping stones towards the Early Learning Goals (QCA), but can be applied equally well to the documents on pre-school education published for Scotland, Wales and Northern Ireland. The activities cover all six Areas of Learning (Personal, social and emotional development, Communication, language and literacy, Mathematical development, Knowledge and understanding of the world, Creative development and Physical development).

## Themes

Themes are often used as a focus for activities. The subjects of 'Clothes' and 'Food', both familiar to young children, are used for this book. Using a wide variety of situations, the range of texts and activities build on the children's existing knowledge, providing some familiar experiences and extending their learning about the world around them.

## Using an anthology

Young children love stories, rhymes, poems and songs. This anthology provides opportunities for them to interact, repeating words and phrases in the songs and rhymes, and to listen in group situations as the stories are read. Information texts are provided to extend the children's understanding of the subjects looked at.

The activities will develop children's thinking and reasoning skills, encouraging them read the texts carefully and to ask questions to extend their understanding.

## Early Learning Goals

This book is designed to assist the planning process and has a range of ideas for developing the children's skills and understanding, while helping them to work towards the Early Learning Goals.

Activities within the book cater for a wide range of abilities. You can therefore select the activities that are most appropriate to the skills and abilities of the children in your own group.

## How to use this book

You can use the activities contained within this book independently, as one-off sessions, or as part of an integrated plan. They should be used as part of everyday play and learning experiences, with oral language as the main focus.

Resources are easily obtainable and the photocopiable pages may be used to extend and reinforce the children's learning. Care should be taken to ensure the safety of the children at all times by checking for dietary requirements, allergies and any other specific individual needs.

# Boots and shoes

(Action rhyme)

These are the big boots
*(stamp feet)*
Uncle Bill wears,
Going thumpity thump –
When he's climbing the stairs.

These are football boots,
*(kicking action)*
Sam kicks the ball.
Whack! It goes –
Right over the wall!

These are Jo's trainers
*(run on the spot)*
bouncy and new.
Running so fast –
She'll soon catch you!

These are my slippers
*(shuffle feet)*
Slip slop they go,
Down at the heel
With a hole in the toe.

These are ballet shoes,
*(on toes and twirl round)*
Up on my toes!
Round and round
the dancer goes.

These are the bootees
*(whisper this verse holding up imaginary bootees)*
On baby's feet.
Not a sound
Just soft and sweet!

Val Jeans-Jakobsson

**Early years wishing well: Clothes and food**

# Boots and shoes

## Personal, social and emotional

★ Talk about activities that the children like doing and discuss whether they require special footwear.

★ Compare the different things that people like to do. Encourage the children to recognize that it is acceptable for people to like different things.

## Communication, language and literacy

★ Make a collection of different types of shoes such as wellington boots, trainers and so on. Label them by writing the name of the shoe on a card and displaying these labels next to the corresponding shoes. Encourage the children to become familiar with the words by discussing the shoes and reading the labels.

★ Introduce new vocabulary to the children such as 'sole', 'tongue', 'eyelet' and 'lace'. Point to the correct part of the shoe as you say the word. Draw a large shoe shape on a display board and ask the children to help you label each part of the shoe.

## Mathematical development

★ Use the positional language in the rhyme to help the children understand the concept of over, down, on and so on. During physical play, challenge the children to crawl under a bench, for example, or climb down the climbing frame.

★ Use routine activities to extend and consolidate these concepts. For example,

when playing with small-world farm animals, talk about the sheep being in the field, the ducks swimming on the pond and so on.

★ Compare the sizes of the children's shoes. Ask the children to draw around their shoes using chalk on black paper. Help each child to cut their shapes out and write the size and their name on each. Display all the footprints along the wall with the sizes increasing.

## Knowledge and understanding of the world

★ Use your collection of shoes and boots to look at their similarities.

★ Talk about features such as studs on the bottom of football boots, and their purpose.

## Physical development

★ Take large sponge balls or blown-up balls that are not too heavy outside. Let the children kick them over objects, through hoops or into a goal. Encourage them to control the ball and to kick it carefully.

## Creative development

★ Look at the different patterns on the soles of the children's shoes and talk about the shapes that you can see. Make rubbings of the soles using wax crayons.

★ Encourage the children to tread in puddles and make footprints on concrete.

★ If you have the opportunity to make tracks in snow, encourage the children to match the prints to the shoes that made them.

# Odd socks in the morning

A spotty sock,
a spotty sock
with half-a-dozen holes.

A silly sock,
a silly sock
with little mice and moles.

A soggy sock,
a soggy sock.
Oh no! It's Baby Joe's!

A smelly sock,
a smelly sock
that makes me hold my nose.

Wes Magee

**SCHOLASTIC** *photocopiable*

**Early years wishing well: Clothes and food**

# Odd socks in the morning

## Personal, social and emotional development

★ The person in the poem is trying to find socks that match. Ask the children if they have ever lost anything and what it felt like. Talk about how they felt when they eventually found the lost article.

★ Talk to the children about taking care of their own property and the group's property and how missing pieces from games or jigsaws spoil their play.

## Communication, language and literacy

★ Put a clean wet sock into a bag and invite the children to guess what is inside the bag by feeling through it. Encourage them to talk about how it feels, and record their words on a large sock shape. Hang up the shape for all the children to see.

★ This activity could be repeated by using objects of different shapes and textures.

## Mathematical development

★ Make a pile of socks and ask the children to match them and put them in pairs.

★ Count how many pairs of socks have been made. This could be recorded using pictures.

★ Sort the socks into sets by colour, pattern, size and length.

★ Cut sock shapes out of coloured card and peg them on a washing line to form a pattern – for example, red sock, blue sock, red sock and so on.

## Knowledge and understanding of the world

★ Have examples of socks worn for different purposes, such as sport socks, frilly party socks, tights for the cold, and thin summer socks. Discuss when the different types of socks would be worn and why.

★ Ask the children whether they wear socks all the time and to talk about why they would not wear them for paddling, walking in the sand and so on.

## Physical development

★ Using the water tray or bowls of soapy water, invite the children to wash socks, rinse them out, squeeze the water out and peg them on a line to dry. Use socks that are already clean so that the children are just familiarizing themselves with the washing process.

★ At the start of a movement session, ask the children to take off their socks and shoes, and to put them back on at the end of the session. Encourage them to discuss how it feels to move around on bare feet – do they like feeling the floor? Is it cold or warm?

## Creative development

★ Design patterns for pairs of socks using paint, crayons or felt-tipped pens.

★ Make puppets by gluing features onto the toe area of socks. Then encourage the children to make up their own stories using the puppets.

# Coats

I've a play coat for the garden
and my best coat's navy blue.

I have a coat with buttons
and a coat that zips-up, too.

I like to wear my anorak
which has a little hood.

But if I wear my cuddly fleece
I feel so snugly good!

Brenda Williams

**Early years wishing well: Clothes and food**

# Coats

## Personal, social and emotional development

★ Ask each child if they have a favourite coat and, if so, why it is special. Encourage them to draw a picture of themselves wearing their favourite coat.

★ Invite the children to help one another to fasten their zips or buttons as they prepare to go outside.

## Communication, language and literacy

★ Make a list of all the different types of coats that the children can think of, such as duffle-coat, anorak, cagoule, parka or raincoat. Invite the children to say the initial letter of each word.

★ Write the rhyming words from the poem down next to each other on a large sheet of paper or a whiteboard. Ask the children if they can think of any more words that rhyme with them. Scribe the new words on the list for the children, or let them add them themselves if they are able.

## Mathematical development

★ Look at the size and shape of a selection of buttons in a tray. Ask the children to sort the buttons into sets of large and small or into different colours.

★ Give each child a copy of the photocopiable sheet on page 78. Encourage them to count the buttons and fill in the boxes with the correct numbers.

## Knowledge and understanding of the world

★ Provide a selection of absorbent and waterproof fabrics and explain that you are going to try to find out which material would be most suitable for a raincoat. Invite the children to offer suggestions as to how to do this. Put a small piece of each material on top of kitchen paper. Add drops of water to the material. Look at which materials let the water through and which the water stays on the top of. Ask the children to decide which material they think would be the best for making raincoats and to explain their choice.

★ Think about different types of weather and make a weather chart with pictures for the weather on each day of the week.

## Physical development

★ Encourage the development of the fine manipulative skills required to do up coats by giving the children inset jigsaws or peg boards to play with.

★ Practise movements to represent different types of weather, such as wiggling fingers for rain and swishing arms for wind.

## Creative development

★ Use painted buttons as a decoration for a photograph or picture frame.

★ Make collage pictures of different coats. Use materials such as pieces of wool fabric for winter coats, Cellophane for rain coats and cotton wool for fleeces.

# This is the hat

 (Action rhyme)

Here are the needles shiny and blue,
That knitted the hat I made for you.    *(knitting action)*

Here is the wool wound up in a ball,    *(describe big and small with
First it was big and now it is small.    hands)*

Here is the sheep on top of the hill,    *(make a 'sheep' with fingers
Whose wool was cut and sent to the mill.    for legs)*

So here is the hat I knitted for you,    *(pretend to put hat on
Put it on now – 'cos your nose is blue!    neighbouring child)*

AND DON'T LOSE IT!    *(wag finger!)*

Val Jeans-Jakobsson

# This is the hat

## Personal, social and emotional development

★ Ask the children to think about clothes that keep us warm and how they would feel if they didn't have them.

★ The hat in the poem was hand-knitted for the child. Ask if any of the children's relatives can knit. Perhaps they could show the children how it is done.

★ Find out if any of the children have ever had any clothes specially knitted for them and talk about how it made them feel.

## Communication, language and literacy

★ On a sheet of paper, make a list of the items that were used to make the hat (sheep's wool, blue knitting needles and ball of wool). Laminate the list and encourage the children to practise their pencil control by writing over the words using a felt-tipped pen, then wiping this off so they can repeat the activity.

★ Show the children pictures of the items corresponding to the words on the list from the previous activity and help them to point out the correct words.

## Mathematical development

★ Discuss why the ball of wool in the poem is getting smaller. Encourage the children to recognize that there is less wool than there was because some of it has been used. Make balls out of Plasticine and order them from large to small.

## Knowledge and understanding of the world

★ Explain to the children how the wool from sheep is turned into wool which can be used for knitting.

★ The sheep in the poem provided the wool for the hat. Bring in and talk about other items we get from animals, such as leather for shoes, duck down for pillows, milk for butter and eggs for cooking.

## Physical development

★ Help the children to make woollen pom-poms. Wind wool through two circular pieces of card which have a hole in the middle. Keep winding until the hole is nearly full. Cut the wool at the outside edge and then tie the strands together with a piece of wool between the two cards. Pull off the cards and you will have a pom-pom for the children.

## Creative development

★ Invite the children to glue wool randomly onto a piece of card. Ask them to paint over the top of it and then print onto different types of paper or card. Use this technique to make cards for special occasions.

★ Encourage the children to paint strips of wool. Ask each child to fold a piece of paper in two and help them to pull the wool through the paper so that it leaves a trail of paint behind. Invite the children to use different colours and thickness to produce different effects.

*Early years wishing well: Clothes and food*

# Dressing up

You can be a Pirate,
I will be a Clown,
and Ben can be a Postman
walking round the town.

You can be a Princess,
I will be a Knight,
and Faye can be a Monster
and give us all a fright.

You can be a Spaceman,
I will be a Queen,
and Jack can be a Giant
dressed in red and green.

You can be a Cowboy,
I will be a King,
and Dean can be a Wizard
with a magic ring.

You can be a Doctor,
I will be a Nurse,
and Jo can be a Teacher
reading us this verse.

Wes Magee

**Early years wishing well: Clothes and food**

# Dressing up

## Personal, social and emotional development

★ The children in the poem are obviously having fun. Talk about the things the children enjoy. It might be going somewhere, having a particular food to eat or playing with their favourite toys.

★ The poem talks about monsters giving you a fright. Discuss frightening things with the children and invite them to tell you how it feels to be frightened.

## Communication, language and literacy

★ Explain that the poem has rhyming words in it. Give the children an example of what you mean by a rhyming word. Go through the poem again and encourage the children to point out the rhyming words.

★ Ask the children if they can think of other rhyming words. Scribe the words for them on a flip chart and make them into a class poem.

## Mathematical development

★ Show the children a collection of envelopes that have been delivered to you. Ask them if they can see any numbers written on the envelopes. Discuss with the group why they are there and how they help the postperson when they sort and deliver people's mail.

★ Invite the children to imagine that they are doing the countdown for the spaceman to take off in his rocket, and help them to count backwards from ten to zero and 'blast off!'.

## Knowledge and understanding of the world

★ Display a selection of books which show different people's work roles. Talk about what a spaceman, doctor or nurse would do and the equipment they would need to use.

★ Invite a local postal delivery worker into your setting so that they can talk about their work or arrange to visit the local post office.

★ Change the role-play area into a post office so that the children can re-create what they saw (if you managed to organize a visit to the post office). Christmas would be a good time to do this so that the children can write their letters to Santa or post Christmas cards to one another.

## Physical development

★ Talk about the various characters in the poem and encourage the children to mime suitable actions for them.

★ Use clothes from your role-play area to play a game, racing to put on outfits as quickly as possible.

## Creative development

★ Invite the children to use old boxes and cylinders to make a model spaceship for a spaceman to travel in.

★ Provide dressing-up clothes for the children to role-play being characters from the poem, or any other characters of their choice.

★ Encourage the children to draw pictures of themselves as characters from the poem.

# Inside out

Push your legs in your sleeves,
Pull your trousers on your head;
Wear your hat on your knees,
Squeeze your wellies on in bed!

Wrap your hands in your socks,
Put your gloves on your toes;
Hang your pants from your ears,
Tie a ribbon on your nose!

Judith Nicholls

**Early years wishing well: Clothes and food**

# Inside out

## Personal, social and emotional development

★ Give the children a range of clothing in a suitcase, with some of the items turned inside out. Challenge groups of two or three children to help one another to dress for a particular occasion such as a party or a game of football. Explain that they will need to help each other with fastenings and so on.

## Communication, language and literacy

★ Explain that the instructions in the poem are the opposite to how it should be done. Talk about how the clothes should be put on instead and where they should be worn.

★ Ask the children if they know the opposites of a variety of words such as up/down, in/out, top/bottom, hard/soft and so on.

## Mathematical development

★ Mix up a variety of small plastic shapes, buttons, animals, vehicles and so on, to use for sorting. Encourage the children to sort the items into separate containers.

★ Play a game called 'I know my numbers inside out'. Prepare a set of number cards numbered 1–10 and a collection of small items of clothing, such as hats, gloves and socks. Lay the cards face down and ask each child to turn a card over and match the correct amount of one type of clothing. If there are not enough items of any type of clothing for a child to take a turn, that child is out of the game.

## Knowledge and understanding of the world

★ Discuss the different types of materials that the clothes in the poem were made from and why.

★ Investigate with the children some of the clothing worn by people who work outside, such as road sweepers, builders and gardeners. Talk about protective and fluorescent clothing.

## Physical development

★ Turn coats inside out and encourage the children to turn them the right way out before putting them on.

★ Use wheeled toys to encourage the children to push and pull with control. Talk about how they would use pushing and pulling movements when they dress – for example, pulling their wellington boots over their feet and legs with their hands.

★ Discuss how trolleys often move better if one person pushes and another pulls. Let the children experiment with ways to make it easier for a person to push or pull a trolley.

## Creative development

★ Encourage the children to make up other nonsense rhymes, perhaps in the style of Edward Lear.

★ Accompany the poem with musical instruments. Invite the children to choose a particular instrument to represent each part of the body or piece of clothing.

*Early years wishing well:* **Clothes and food**

# The sun-hat

The sun was blazing down onto the beach. The sea was sparkling. Ben's mum and dad lay back in their deckchairs and watched Ben building a big sand-castle.

'Ben,' called his mum, 'it's very hot. Put your sun-hat on.'

Sun-hat? Where is it? Ben wondered.

Then he saw it poking out of a heap of sand. He pulled it out and plonked it on his head. Ben didn't like his sun-hat. He knew he should always wear one when the sun was hot, but he'd had this one since he was very small. It had blue elephants over it and looked silly.

When Ben's sand-castle was finished, he picked up his bucket.

'I'm just going to get some water for the moat,' he said.

'Okay,' said his dad. 'Stay in the shallow water. I'll watch you.'

Ben filled his bucket to the top. Then he saw some lovely, smooth pebbles.

'They'd look nice round my castle,' he said.

His bucket was full of water, so Ben put the pebbles in his sun-hat instead. He walked slowly back with his bucket in one hand and his sun-hat in the other.

'Ben!' said his mum. 'That hat should be on your head!'

Later, they all went exploring rock pools. Ben spotted a little crab. When his mum and dad weren't looking, Ben scooped it up with his sun-hat, so he could have a closer look. It was brilliant. Carefully, he put the hat back into the pool and the crab scurried under a rock.

'Ben!' said his mum. 'That hat should be on your head!'

Ben put on his wet hat. It was lovely and cool!

Later still, everyone was hungry.

'Come on, Ben,' said his dad. 'Let's see what we can find to eat.'

They bought hot dogs, apple pies, cans of drink and some juicy peaches.

'I can't carry all this!' said Dad.

'I'll help,' said Ben. He put the hot dogs and apple pies inside his sun-hat.

When they got back, Ben's mum frowned.

'Ben!' she said. 'That hat should be *on your head!*'

'It's my fault,' said his dad, laughing. 'Come on, Ben. I think it's time we got you a new sun-hat.'

Ben's new sun-hat was bright red. It had a peak at the front and a flap at the back.

'Ace!' cheered Ben. 'But I think I'll keep my old hat as well. It's *very useful!*'

Patricia Leighton

**Early years wishing well: Clothes and food**

# The sun-hat

## Personal, social and emotional development

★ Ask the children why Ben should have kept his hat on. Talk about the things we sometimes do that we should not do. Emphasize to the children that we all need to consider how our actions may be harmful to ourselves or hurtful to others.

★ Discuss with the children the things that they enjoy doing with their families.

## Communication, language and literacy

★ Talk about the children's visits to the seaside. Discuss how they got there, what they wore and what they did during the visit. Ask each child to draw or paint a picture of themselves at the seaside and make all the pictures into a book, scribing the children's comments for the captions.

★ Ask the children if any of them have ever had fun writing in the wet sand on the beach. Dampen the sand in the sand tray and encourage the children to write their names or make patterns in it.

## Mathematical development

★ Draw some starfish or sharks on a whiteboard and encourage the children to count the number of legs on the starfish and fins on the shark with you.

★ Talk about two starfish having more legs than just one starfish. Draw two and count the legs with the children.

★ Put shells in the sand and order them, starting with the largest and ending with the smallest, or make a repeating pattern.

## Knowledge and understanding of the world

★ Ask the children how they protect themselves from the sun when they are at the seaside or playing outside. Talk about how suncream, sun-hats, parasols and sun-glasses all protect them from the sun.

★ Give each child a copy of the photocopiable sheet on page 79 and ask them to draw a line to match each form of sun protection to the person they think it belongs to.

## Physical development

★ Mime digging a hole on the beach. Encourage the children to think about how they feel when they are doing a strenuous activity on a hot day, then ask them to show that they are hot and tired in their mime.

★ Go outside on a sunny day and play shadow-jumping. The children should try to jump on each other's shadows, saying the name of the person the shadow belongs to as they do it.

## Creative development

★ Put a selection of objects in the sand tray, such as small dolls, dolls' hats, small umbrellas, shells, small buckets and spades and flags. Encourage the children to use them to create a beach scene.

**Early years wishing well: Clothes and food**

# Auntie Parminder's wedding

The rolls of silk were all the colours of the rainbow. Jasminder didn't know which to choose for her suit for Auntie Parminder's wedding. Her mum's was going to be blue and silver. Jasminder finally decided on silver and lilac.

She couldn't wait to see how it would look made up.

When their suits were ready, Jasminder and her mum tried them on. They were perfect. Mum's lenghar suit had a tunic and long skirt, while Jasminder's Punjabi suit had a tunic and trousers. Jasminder did a twirl in front of the long mirror, then held Mum's silky, see-through chuni over her face.

'Look!' she cried. 'I'm a grown-up lady like you!'

Dad smiled at them. 'You both look like princesses,' he said.

The night before the wedding, Auntie Parminder held a party at her house for the ladies and girls who were her friends and family. They all wore their prettiest clothes. Auntie Parminder had beautiful, golden-brown patterns painted on her hands and feet with henna paste. Some of her English friends wore special Indian clothes, too, and joined in all the dancing, clapping and singing. It was a lovely party.

Next morning, Jasminder and her parents got up early, showered and dressed for the wedding. Jasminder put on silver sandals and gold and silver bangles to match her new suit. Mum wore her new outfit and best jewellery, and Dad put on his best suit and a neat turban.

At the gurdwara, Auntie Parminder wore a beautiful red and gold sari and chuni, and gold wedding jewellery.

After the wedding, there was another party – this time for everyone – with delicious food and a wedding cake with thick, white icing. The men all danced when the drummer played the big dohl, then the women and girls all danced to the disco.

But when the time came for Auntie Parminder to leave with Uncle Jaspal, the man she had married, most of her friends and family were in tears. Even Jasminder's mum was laughing and crying at the same time.

'Why is everyone crying?' asked Jasminder.

'It's because she is leaving home,' Auntie Janice explained. 'Auntie Parminder will be living with Uncle Jaspal now, in her own home.'

Cousin Sital rolled his eyes at Jasminder. 'She's only going to live four doors down the road!' he told her.

As the happy bride and groom drove away to waving and cheering, Jasminder shrugged. 'Grown-ups are very hard to understand, sometimes!' she said.

---

### Glossary

*Chuni: long, transparent scarf, worn by Punjabi women (but not young girls) to cover their hair in public.*
*Gurdwara: Sikh temple.*
*Dohl: large drum used to accompany banghra dancing.*

Barbara Moore

**Early years wishing well: Clothes and food**

# Auntie Parminder's wedding

## Personal, social and emotional development

★ Discuss any weddings or celebrations that the children have been to and talk about the special foods that were eaten and clothes that were worn.

★ In the story, Auntie Parminder is going to live somewhere else even though it is near to her family. Talk about moving house, all the things you have to do and all the changes that happen. Talk about making friends and how the children could help someone who was new to settle in. This could be a useful activity if you have a new child in your setting.

## Communication, language and literacy

★ Look at the Indian words in the story. Talk about different people speaking different languages. If there is a child in your group who is learning English as a second language, ask them to teach the other children to say 'Hello' or 'Goodbye' in their first language.

★ Tell the children that some languages are written and read differently from English. Ask them to point to words as you read a caption so that they begin to realize that English is read from left to right and top to bottom.

## Mathematical development

★ Look at a selection of square and rectangular scarves. Look at the sides of a square scarf – do the children notice anything about them? Measure the sides with string or a measuring tape. This can be repeated with the rectangular scarves.

★ Ask the children to describe the pattern on their clothes using shape vocabulary.

★ Use cars, coloured bricks, shapes or cups and plates to make patterns. Invite each child to continue them, or start patterns for a partner to copy. Give each child a copy of the photocopiable sheet on page 80 and ask them to continue the patterns.

## Knowledge and understanding of the world

★ Show the children pictures of the clothing mentioned in the story. If a child at your setting has relatives that wear saris, invite them to visit your setting and show the children how the sari is worn.

## Physical development

★ Play Indian music to the children. Give them silk scarves and encourage them to use these to move to the music.

## Creative development

★ Invite the children to create their own designs for patterns on their hands. Buy wash-off henna or body paints and help the children to copy their designs onto their own or each other's hands.

★ Using fabric paints and fine cotton cloth, make a Chuni with the children. (If the cloth is washed first and ironed afterwards, it can be washed and the pattern will not be removed.)

# Evie's uniform

'Right, Evie, time to get dressed,' said Mum, one morning. 'What do you want to wear?'

Evie looked at all the clothes hanging in her wardrobe. 'I don't know,' she sighed. She wished she had special clothes to wear, like Mum, Dad and James. Mum always wore a grey skirt, grey jacket and a pink striped blouse. She worked in a big shop in town and everyone who worked there wore the same clothes. Mum said it was the shop's *uniform*. James always wore a white shirt, black trousers, grey jumper and a tie, like all the other boys at his school. James said it was the school's *uniform*.

Dad always wore blue overalls. He worked in a garage and everyone wore overalls to keep their clothes clean. The name of the garage was embroidered on the top pocket. Dad said it was their *uniform*.

Everyone had a uniform to wear, except Evie. So no one else ever had trouble deciding what to wear.

Mum searched through Evie's wardrobe and took out a pretty yellow dress.

'I don't want to wear that,' Evie began to protest, but Mum was already unbuttoning her pyjama top. 'Oh, come on, Evie, we'll be late!'

First, Mum dropped James off at school then she took Evie to Nanny's. She looked after Evie every morning while Mum went to work. Evie loved going to Nanny's. They always did lots of interesting things.

Today, they did some painting. Evie splashed some red paint on her dress, but Nanny said it didn't matter.

Then they went to the park. Evie played on the swings and slide. She got some mud on her dress, but Nanny said it didn't matter.

Then they went shopping and Nanny bought Evie an ice-cream. Soon there was ice-cream as well as mud and red paint on Evie's pretty yellow dress.

'I know what you need,' said Nanny.

She took Evie to a clothes shop and bought her two pairs of red dungarees and two red-and-white striped jumpers.

'You can wear these clothes every morning when you come to my house,' Nanny told Evie. 'Then you can play without worrying about messing up your clothes.'

'Like a uniform?' asked Evie.

'That's right,' smiled Nanny. 'This is your "playing at Nanny's" uniform.'

'Thanks, Nanny!' Evie smiled happily. Now Evie had special clothes to wear every morning just like Mum, Dad and James and she never had trouble deciding what to wear again.

Karen King

# Evie's uniform

## Personal, social and emotional development

★ Evie's Nanny was not cross when Evie got messy but the children may have experienced adults being cross when they have got in a mess. Discuss why people sometimes get cross. Remind the group that if people are cross, it does not mean that they will not forgive them.

★ Talk to the children about men and women being able to do various work roles. Use a variety of non-stereotypical books and pictures to reinforce this.

## Communication, language and literacy

★ Ask the children if they know anyone who wears a uniform, and encourage them to describe it.

★ Grandparents are often given different names. Make a list of what the children call their grandmothers and grandfathers.

★ Invite the children to bring in photographs of themselves with their grandparents and encourage them to help you make these into a group book. The children could write, or you could scribe, using the children's vocabulary, a sentence about what they like doing with their grandparents, as captions to accompany the photographs.

## Mathematical development

★ Make small cakes for the children to take home for older family members. Give each child copies of the instructions on the photocopiable sheets on pages 81 and 82. Offer close adult supervision and work in small groups to carry out the recipe.

## Knowledge and understanding of the world

★ Invite a firefighter or the local crossing-patrol person to your setting to talk about their uniform and why they need to wear it.

★ Copy the photocopiable sheets on pages 83 and 84, laminate them and cut out the individual pieces. Give each child in a group of six one of the character cards from the photocopiable sheet on page 84 and lay the item cards from the photocopiable sheet on page 83 face down in the centre of the group. Ask each child to turn over an item card. If the clothing matches their character, they keep the card; if not, they turn it back over and play continues. The first person to collect the full set of uniform items wins.

## Physical development

★ Visit a local park so that the children can use the swings and the slide.

★ Play a game seeing who can put on and take off an old pair of dungarees the fastest.

## Creative development

★ Talk about the benefits for groups of people to have clothes that identify them. Ask the children to help you design a T-shirt or sweatshirt for your group.

# The washing machine

'Goodness me!' said Mrs Rabbit, looking out of the window. 'What's that?'

Four weasels were carrying a large brown box up the garden path. 'Oh,' said Mr Rabbit, 'that must be the new washing machine. Um... there was a special offer at Weasel's Warehouse.'

'A *washing machine*?' said Mrs Rabbit. 'Oh, my. I just hope you know how to use it, Mr Rabbit!'

'Oh, I'm sure it will be simple,' said Mr Rabbit confidently.

The weasels unpacked the machine and connected up the pipes for them. Then they went off in their van without a word.

The rabbits stared at the gleaming appliance. They pulled out the little drawer at the top, twirled all the knobs and opened and closed the door.

'I think we need to read the instruction book,' said Mr Rabbit.

'We'll fetch some things that need washing,' said the twins, Daisy and Dill. 'Er... maybe we should just do a few things at first,' said Mr Rabbit when he saw the heaps of washing all around him. 'The book says you have to sort everything.'

'Oh,' said Mrs Rabbit. 'Well, Dill – you put yours in first.'

Dill put his socks, pants, T-shirts, jumpers and jeans into the machine. There was just room for him to squeeze in his trainers.

'Now, we need washing powder,' said Mr Rabbit.

'How about this?' asked Mrs Rabbit, handing him a box. 'It cleans the bath ever so well.'

Mr Rabbit filled the little drawer with powder and pushed it back in. 'Now... 'SELECT WASH PROGRAMME'... er... probably number one should do it. It is the first wash, after all.'

The washing machine sprang to life and all Dill's things started going round and round.

Fascinated, the rabbits watched. And watched. And watched.

One by one they fell asleep.

Bubbles started appearing round the door of the machine. A sea of foam crept across the kitchen.

Daisy and Dill, curled up on the floor, might have been lost for good if Mrs Hedgehog from next door hadn't called round to borrow some tea!

She helped them clean up the kitchen and empty the machine. All Dill's washing came out a kind of pinky-bluey-grey colour. Even his trainers. And his jumpers were about the right size for mice.

Mrs Hedgehog had to explain all about sorting clothes into hot wash and cool wash, whites and colours, and about using the right kind of powder.

A week later, she had tea with Mrs Rabbit.

'And how's the new washing machine?' she asked.

'Oh, we don't use it very much,' said Mrs Rabbit, a bit awkwardly. 'Only when there's nothing on television.'

Jackie Andrews

**Early years wishing well: Clothes and food**

# The washing machine

## Personal, social and emotional development

★ Ask the children who they would ask for help if they needed it. Talk about how they can help one another by working together as they construct things or complete jigsaws.

## Communication, language and literacy

★ Talk about different types of books, leaflets and posters that provide information in the same way as the instruction book would have helped the rabbits. Display different examples of information texts for the children to look at.

★ Invite the children to look at the care labels in their clothes and explain the information that they offer. Talk about other types of symbols that inform us, such as road signs, musical notes and ticks and crosses.

★ Work together to create an instruction leaflet with pictures and/or writing that give instructions on using a favourite toy or piece of equipment in your setting.

## Mathematical development

★ Think about the circular shapes that are found on a washing machine and encourage the children to look for circles in the room.

★ Ask the children to bring some circular packaging from home, to help make washing machines and dryers for the role-play area. Talk about the different numbers that are found on washing machines and what they tell us. Encourage the children to add numbers to their washing machines to indicate different temperatures. (The numbers do not need to represent washing temperatures!)

## Knowledge and understanding of the world

★ Bring a piece of dry-cleaned clothing to your setting on its hanger in its plastic bag. Discuss how clothes are pressed, put on hangers and covered with a plastic bag so that they do not get creased or dirty. Reinforce the safety rules associated with plastic bags.

★ Experiment with different ways of drying washing – for example, put clothes outside in different types of weather and make a note of how well they dry.

## Physical development

★ Encourage the children to help you reorganize the role-play area into a launderette. The children will need to carry, push and pull and be aware of space as they manoeuvre the props. Show them how to pick things up carefully by bending their knees.

## Creative development

★ Talk about how clothes fade when they have been washed a lot. Experiment with mixing paint to get different shades. Let the children paint 'before' and 'after' pictures of new and faded clothes.

★ Provide a selection of fabrics and invite the children to make a collage of a scene from the story using real fabric to show the clothes.

# A dress for a special day

My big sister, Marie, was going to make her first Holy Communion at church. Mum's friend, Jane, was going to make her white dress for her.

First, though, Marie had to be measured.

Round we went to Jane's house. I took my doll, Rosy, as well.

Jane took out her tape measure and held it round Marie's chest. Then she measured round Marie's middle, and lastly she measured from Marie's neck, all down her back, to just below her knees. She wrote all the measurements on a piece of paper.

I thought Rosy would like to be measured as well, so Jane wrote down all Rosy's measurements, too.

The very next Saturday, we went to the shop that sold dress patterns and fabrics. Marie looked in the big pattern books for something she liked.

Next we had to choose the fabric. Marie picked a white cotton with little embroidered flowers. Mum called it broderie anglaise. She took the roll to the counter to be measured and cut, and finally bought a reel of thread and a zip. We took it all round to Jane.

She cleared a large space on the living-room floor and put down a big piece of card. This was her cutting-out board. She lay the fabric down on the board, smoothing it out to make sure there were no creases.

Next, Jane pinned the pattern pieces to the fabric. Then she cut round them with huge pair of scissors. It was scary – but Jane didn't make any mistakes!

It was all ready for Jane to sew.

A few days later, Marie had to go and try it on. Jane had just tacked the pieces together with large stitches. She checked to see if it fitted Marie. Then she pinned up the hem to the right length.

The dress already looked very pretty.

Just before Marie's special day, we went to collect her finished dress. It was hanging on Jane's wardrobe, wrapped in a plastic bag. It looked beautiful. And Jane had made a headband out of white and blue silk flowers to go with it.

But there was one more surprise. Hanging on a tiny coat-hanger next to it was a *very small* dress made from the pieces of material that were left over – and it was just the right size for Rosy!

Marie's special day turned out to be a special day for Rosy and me, too!

Jackie Andrews

**Early years wishing well: Clothes and food**

# A dress for a special day

## Personal, social and emotional development

★ Some children may have family members who have made their first Holy Communion. Talk about where it happened, who took part and what everyone did.

★ Invite a vicar, priest, rabbi or any other religious leader to your setting to talk about some of the special events that they celebrate and the clothes that are worn for them.

★ Talk about other special events that have happened in the children's lives.

## Communication, language and literacy

★ Discuss occasions when people dress up, such as birthday parties and weddings. Ask the children to bring in photographs to inspire discussion. Display these with captions and relevant information books after you have talked about them.

★ Provide the children with outlines of different items of clothing, and ask them to fill the blank clothes with repeating patterns.

## Mathematical development

★ Compare the sizes of the children's clothes, talking about them being bigger, smaller, longer or shorter.

★ Look at the labels in the children's clothes to find their sizes (these might be age or height sizes). Talk to the children about what the figures mean. Ask them to find the same numerals on a number line.

★ Provide the children with tape measures. Invite them to pair up and encourage them to try measuring different parts of each other's bodies.

## Knowledge and understanding of the world

★ Take the children for a walk around your locality to look at special buildings. Talk with the group about what the buildings are and what happens in them.

★ Make a simple model village using recycled materials for the buildings. This will encourage the children to identify features in their local environment. The group could use the village for their imaginative play, taking cars, buses and people into the village and re-creating roles.

## Physical development

★ Invite the children to practise simple sewing using laces and beads or hole-punched cards.

★ Prepare a selection of special clothes, hats and bags for the children to dress up in or to dress their dolls in.

## Creative development

★ Make collage pictures using a variety of fabrics and textures that the children can cut and glue. Encourage the group to describe the different patterns and textures.

★ Invite the children to make peg dolls using wooden clothes pegs, scraps of material, wool, felt-tipped pens and fabric glue.

# Great Grandma's washing day

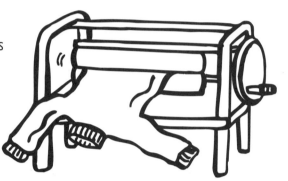

A long, long time ago, when Great Grandma was a little girl, Mondays meant *washing day*.

It was not easy to wash and dry clothes in those days, for they didn't have washing machines or tumble-dryers.

First of all, they had to light a fire underneath a large, brick boiler that was filled with water and soap flakes. Great Grandma had to help her mother scrub the dirty marks out of the clothes on a wooden board, and bash them up and down in the water with a special stick called a 'dolly'. Then all the white washing – sheets, towels and cotton petticoats – were left to boil clean.

All the woollen clothes had to be washed carefully by hand in the sink, rinsed in cold water and put through the mangle.

The huge mangle, with wooden rollers, stood in the corner of the wash-house. Great Grandma's mother lifted the clothes from the boiler with a wooden stick, and dropped them into a tin bath. The mangle would squeeze out the water. Great Grandma had to turn the handle while her mother smoothed the clothes through the rollers. It was hard work and they both got very wet.

The clothes all had to be rinsed in cold water and mangled again.

After this, sheets, table-cloths and white clothes were soaked in a special blue rinsing water to make them even whiter. Then they were mangled again.

The clothes were hung out to dry on a long washing line, with wooden pegs. If it was raining, they had to dry the washing on lines over the fire in the kitchen, or on a folding wooden frame called a clothes horse. Everywhere was damp and steamy, and everyone got cross.

There was no hot dinner on Monday. Only cold meat left over from Sunday, or bread and cheese.

Great Grandma was very glad when washing day was over. But she sometimes had a bowl of soapy water and a white clay pipe to play with – and she would sit on the doorstep blowing bubbles with them!

Margaret Willetts

**Early years wishing well: Clothes and food**

# Great Grandma's washing day

## Personal, social and emotional development

★ Talk about children having to work as many would have done in Great Grandma's lifetime.

★ Even though Great Grandma was a child, she had to help with the chores in the house. Talk about the jobs that the children help out with around the house, such as tidying up their toys or putting the shopping away.

## Communication, language and literacy

★ There are many words in the text that the children will be unfamiliar with, such as 'dolly', 'mangle' and 'clothes horse'. Show the children pictures of these items or see if your local library or museum has an artefacts loan scheme so that the children can look at real examples.

## Mathematical development

★ In the text, it took all day to do the washing. Talk about time and how long it takes the children to do certain things. You could make this into a game by asking the children to tidy away their toys by the time you have counted to ten.

★ Ask the children what Great Grandma had to do first, second and so on. Talk about the order we do the washing in: first, we get the clothes out of the basket; second, we sort them into dark and pale colours, and so on.

★ Invite the children to stand in a line and point out first, second, third and so on.

## Knowledge and understanding of the world

★ Discuss the machinery we use today for washing and drying clothes. Introduce the children to the difference between automatic washing machines and washing the clothes manually or by hand.

★ Ask the children if they think Great Grandma would have worn the same type of clothes as they do. Make a collection of old photographs showing the clothes worn by their parents, grandparents and great grandparents.

★ Look at other changes that have taken place in households, such as the change from coal fires to central heating and the use of vacuum cleaners rather than manual tools such as carpet beaters.

## Physical development

★ Invite the children to play some Victorian games such as 'Spinning top', 'Hopscotch' and skipping games.

★ Encourage the children to mime the actions of washing and drying clothes in the way Great Grandma would have.

## Creative development

★ Provide the children with an old white sheet for them to splatter paint onto.

★ Have a Victorian day where the adults and children dress up in Victorian-style clothing. You could turn part of your room into a Victorian classroom for the day.

# What we wear in my family

(Tune: 'Skip to My Lou')

Steady speed

1. My grand-dad, he wears bra-ces, My grand-dad, he wears bra-ces, My grand-dad, he wears bra-ces, Bra-ces are what my grand-dad wears.

2. My granny, she wears stockings
My granny, she wears stockings
My granny, she wears stockings
Stockings are what my granny wears.

3. My daddy, he wears T-shirts...

4. My mummy, she wears jackets...

5. My brother, he wears trainers...

6. My sister, she wears leggings...

7. Me, I wear pyjamas
Me, I wear pyjamas
Me, I wear pyjamas
When I go to bed (*all shout*) night-night!

Ann Bryant

**Early years wishing well: Clothes and food**

# What we wear in my family

## Personal, social and emotional development

★ The song talks about what various family members wear. Discuss who is in the children's family. Find out the names of relatives and how they are related to the children.

★ Find out if any of the children have a favourite item of clothing. Can they explain why it is special to them?

## Communication, language and literacy

★ Make a display of different types of clothing and label them.

★ Help the children to scribe statements about clothes that members of their families wear, following the same sentence structure used in the song: 'My mummy, she wears…'.

## Mathematical development

★ Use the photocopiable sheet on page 85 to play a matching game. Photocopy the sheet, laminate it and cut out the pieces. Lay them face down in separate groups of characters and clothes. Ask each child to turn over two cards, one from each set. If they match the words of the song, the child keeps that pair.

★ Count how many children are wearing trainers. Make a simple chart to show the numbers of children wearing each type of shoe in your setting.

★ Prepare pictures of the garments mentioned in each verse. Ask the children to help you sort them in to the correct order that they would put them on. Discuss the order using the words 'first', 'second', 'third' and so on.

## Knowledge and understanding of the world

★ Prepare a selection of clothing in a bag or suitcase for differing genders, age ranges and cultures. Ask the children to identify who would wear the clothes and what they would wear them for.

## Physical development

★ Invite the children to mime putting on each item of clothing mentioned in the song.

★ Play a game of swapping coats. Ask the children to wear their coats and work in pairs. They should take off their coats, swap them and put each other's on as quickly as they can before sitting down. The first pair to be seated is the winner.

## Creative development

★ Create new verses to the song using the children's suggestions about members of their own families.

★ Make several copies onto card of the photocopiable sheet on page 86. Glue fabric onto the templates to make the clothing of the different characters in the song. Cut out the characters and attach a length of dowelling rod to the reverse of each so that the children can move the puppets.

★ Perform the song for other children in the group using the puppets.

Clothes Songs

# Getting dressed

(Tune: 'This Old Man')

1. First my pants, Sec-ond my vest, Trou-sers next, Then I'm near-ly dressed.

Now a T-shirt, Which one do I choose? Two striped socks and a pair of shoes.

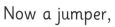

2. First my pants,
Second my vest,
Shalwar kameez, then I'm nearly dressed.
Now a jumper,
Which one do I choose?
Two striped socks and a
Pair of shoes.

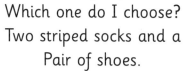

3. First my pants,
Second my vest,
Some more clothes, then I'm nearly dressed.
Putting clothes on,
Such a lot to choose.
Two striped socks and a
Pair of shoes.

Susan Eames

**Early years wishing well: Clothes and food**

# Getting dressed

## Personal, social and emotional development

★ Talk with the children about the things that they are able to do now that they could not do when they were younger, such as dressing themselves, feeding themselves and putting their clothes and toys away. Remind them that they have learnt a lot.

★ Show the children that you value their attempts to dress themselves for outdoor play or messy play.

## Communication, language and literacy

★ Encourage the children to talk about and name different parts of clothing such as sleeves, collars, cuffs and so on.

★ Discuss with the children how they choose what to wear on different days. Do they think about colour they would like to wear? The weather that day? Invite them to describe what they are wearing today.

## Mathematical development

★ Give each child in a group of six a copy of the photocopiable sheet on page 87 and a pair of child-safe scissors. Give them each a number from 1 to 6 and roll a dice. If the dice lands on their number, they can colour in a piece of clothing. When a child has coloured all the clothing on their sheet, they can select an outfit, cut it out and glue it onto their figure.

★ Gather examples of the articles mentioned in the song and mix them up. Ask the children

to fold them up and put them in a pile so that they could be put on quickly. Remind them that the first article to be put on will need to be at the top of the pile, and so on.

## Knowledge and understanding of the world

★ Ask the children to talk about clothes that keep us warm in winter and cool in summer.

★ Put some hot water into several identical containers and wrap these up with different fabrics to see which one retains the heat and keeps the water warm the longest. Explain to the children that this type of fabric would make good winter clothing to keep them warm. Then relate this experiment to the differences between summer clothes and winter clothes.

## Physical development

★ Invite the children to play a game miming putting on different items of clothing while the rest of the group tries to guess what it is.

## Creative development

★ Make up some class poems about getting dressed. Think about what is worn on different parts of the body, the colours or textures that clothes might be and how they are put on. The poems do not need to have rhymes but should use the children's own vocabulary. Write out the final poem and display it with a selection of the children's illustrations mounted around it.

**Early years wishing well: Clothes and food**

# Put on your shirt

1. Put on your shirt and but-ton up, but-ton up, Put on your shirt and but-ton up, but-ton up,

Put on your shirt and but-ton up, but-ton up, When it's the start of the day.

2. Put on your trousers
Pull them up, pull them up
Put on your trousers
Pull them up, pull them up
Put on your trousers
Pull them up, pull them up
When it's the start of the day.

3. Put on your shoes and
Lace them up, lace them up...

4. Put on your coat and
Zip it up, zip it up...

5. Put on your scarf and
Wrap it round, wrap it round
Put on your scarf and
Wrap it round, wrap it round
Put on your scarf and
Wrap it round, wrap it round
Then we can go out to play.

Johanne Levy

**Early years wishing well: Clothes and food**

# Put on your shirt

## Personal, social and emotional development

★ Invite the children to consider what would happen if we tugged at buttons or forced zips when putting on our clothes. Talk with the group about treating things carefully and with consideration.

★ Discuss the importance of playing outside and getting fresh air, even when we need to wrap up warm to do so. Encourage the children to think about how they feel after they have had a good run around outside.

## Communication, language and literacy

★ Make an enlarged copy of the song for the children to look at. Ask them to help you identify repeated words and phrases.

★ Invite the children to think of other items of clothing and the actions they use when putting them on. Scribe their suggestions for them on a sheet of paper that you can stick next to the enlarged song.

## Mathematical development

★ At circle time, ask the children who are wearing shirts to stand up. Count how many there are. Invite those with long-sleeved shirts to move into a separate group. Count the two groups separately and then together again. Encourage the children to count with you at each stage.

★ Repeat the exercise from the previous activity using two hoops, one red and one blue. Invite the children wearing trousers to stand up. If they have zipped trousers, ask them to stand in the red hoop, and if they wear trousers that are elasticated, ask them to stand in the blue hoop.

## Knowledge and understanding of the world

★ Allow the children to experiment with wheeled toys and ramps to gain practical experience of the forces involved in pushing and pulling. Can any of the children tell you whether they need to be behind, in front of, under or above the object in order to push it?

★ Introduce pulleys into the construction apparatus so that the children can experiment with how to pull heavy weights to a higher level. Discuss with the group other lifting apparatus such as cranes.

## Physical development

★ Invite the children to go outside and provide them with large heavy wooden bricks, tyres and planks of wood for them to build with. Teach them about safety and how to lever heavy materials into position.

★ Ask the children to mime the dressing actions mentioned in the song.

## Creative development

★ Encourage the children to use colourful paints, pencils or crayons to create a picture of themselves in their favourite 'playing out' clothes.

# A great big pair of wellington boots

1. A great big pair of wel-ling-ton boots for splash-ing in the wet when the rain comes. A

great big pair of wel-ling-ton boots for splash-ing in the wet when the rain comes.

Let the rain come, I don't care, I need wel-lies and I've got a pair. A

great big pair of wel-ling-ton boots for splash-ing in the wet when the rain comes.

2. A great big woolly, coloured scarf for
Keeping out the cold when the snow
  comes.
A great big woolly, coloured scarf for
Keeping out the cold when the snow
  comes.
Let the snow come I don't care.

My thick scarf'll keep the cold out there.
A great big woolly, coloured scarf for
Keeping out the cold when the snow
  comes.

Clive Barnwell

**Early years wishing well: Clothes and food**

# A great big pair of wellington boots

## Personal, social and emotional development

★ Talk about the pleasure of splashing in the rain wearing wellington boots. Ask the children what their favourite kind of weather is and why.

★ Develop the role-play area into an igloo or snow-castle using plenty of white and silver paper or material. Put gloves, scarves, snow boots, thick coats and skin rugs inside for the children to use. Encourage them to play together and share the clothes.

## Communication, language and literacy

★ Look at words that sound the same but have different meanings, such as pair/pear, bear/bare or see/sea. Ask younger children to say the words with you and encourage them to try to think of any other rhyming pairs. Older children could look at the different spellings of the words and talk about what each version means.

★ Discuss why we wear wellington boots and how they keep us dry. Make a list on a boot-shaped piece of paper of other items of clothing that keep us dry.

## Mathematical development

★ Order sets of objects by size and talk about which is the biggest and which is the smallest.

★ Pair is a way of describing two things that go together. Look at other things that are usually in pairs, such as socks, gloves or shoes. Prepare a collection of gloves or socks for the children to put into pairs.

## Knowledge and understanding of the world

★ Talk about what time of year we have snowy weather. Think about how the roads and pavements can become slippery and explain how the gritter keeps the roads free from snow and ice.

★ Investigate ice with the children. Freeze some water in a balloon or a rubber glove so that the children can see it expand.

## Physical development

★ Let the children practise pulling on wellington boots and taking them off again.

★ Place hoops on the floor and encourage the children to imagine these are puddles, and to jump in and out of them pretending to splash. This could be developed further into a whole mime with the children miming putting on their wellington boots, scarves, hats and so on before going outside to play.

## Creative development

★ Let the children use paints, coloured pencils or crayons to make winter pictures with 'cold' colours such as blue, silver and grey.

★ Encourage the children to make model snowmen using yoghurt cartons, cotton wool, pieces of fabric and sticky paper. If it is near Christmas, a small gift could be put inside for the children to take home.

# Fasteners

(Tune: 'Here We Go Round the Mulberry Bush')

1. But-tons with holes to push them through, Push them through, push them through.

But-tons with holes to push them through And zips to run up and down.

2. Velcro tapes that stick like glue,
   Stick like glue, stick like glue.
   Velcro tapes that stick like glue.
   And zips to run up and down.

3. Buckles with straps to wiggle through...
   And zips to run up and down.

4. Laces for bows to tie your shoe...
   And zips to run up and down.

Sue Nicholls

**Early years wishing well: Clothes and food**

# Fasteners

## Personal, social and emotional development

★ Have an 'I can fasten' as part of the children's records of achievement. Make a chart for each child with simple drawings showing the different types of fasteners – for example, buttons, zips, laces and so on. As they learn how to use each one, let them colour in the corresponding drawing. Praise them for what they can do and encourage them to keep trying at what they still have to achieve.

## Communication, language and literacy

★ Put a fastener into a draw-string bag. Ask a child to feel through the bag and describe its contents. The other children in the group should try to guess the contents of the bag from the child's description.

★ Play with the children a variation of the 'What am I?' game. An adult will need to start this off by describing a fastener – for example, 'I am made of metal. I can be pulled up and down. I am often found on coats and trousers. What am I?' (A zip). Help the children with their clues and encourage them to use descriptive language.

## Mathematical development

★ Prepare a collection of different-shaped buttons and encourage the children to match the circular, triangular, square and rectangular ones to the corresponding shapes that you have drawn on a card. Invite them to count how many buttons there are of each shape.

★ Look at a selection of buttons and notice the different ways that the holes are arranged. Ask the children to count the holes and sort the buttons into sets.

## Knowledge and understanding of the world

★ Make a collection of fasteners for items of clothing, such as zips, hooks and eyes, buttons, laces and velcro. Invite the children to look at what they are made of and to put them into sets of materials, such as plastic, fabric, wood, metal and so on.

★ Use magnets to check whether different zips are magnetic. Can the children move a metallic zip up and down using a magnet?

★ Look at fasteners in the environment – for example, door locks, window catches and magnetic catches on doors.

## Physical development

★ Encourage the children to run, walk and skip up and down an area pretending to be zips, or make their bodies into circular shapes pretending they are buttons.

★ Encourage the children to practise doing up their own fastenings whenever possible.

## Creative development

★ Invite the children to make face collages using a variety of fastenings.

*Early years wishing well: Clothes and food*

# Tell us what you're wearing today

1. Jim-jams, wind-jams, wel-lies in the rain, Shorts and T-shirt rea-dy for games.

Jeans and train-ers, dun-ga-rees for play, Tell us what you're wear-ing to-day.

I like ... I like ... I like ... I like ...

I like ... I like ... These are some of our fa-vour-ite clothes.

2. Scarf and hat and gloves on in the snow,
Coats with hoods in case the winds blow.
Swimming costume, football kit is go
Tell us what's your favourite clothes.
I like...*

3. Fancy dress at parties can be great,
Dress up as a frothy milkshake!
Best clothes, school clothes, clothes to
   go and play
Tell us what you're wearing today.
I like...*

*Children say their favourite clothes.

Peter Morrell

**Early years wishing well: Clothes and food**

# Tell us what you're wearing today

## Personal, social and emotional development

★ Talk about the importance of learning to swim. Ask the children where they go swimming. Do they have lessons or belong to a club? Has anyone gained a swimming certificate? Ask the children what they wear to go swimming and whether they use any equipment, such as goggles or armbands.

★ Have a fancy-dress party and let the children invite their families to join in. Some of the children could act as waiters and waitresses, wearing aprons and taking orders.

## Communication, language and literacy

★ Encourage the children to finish the verses of the song with their own suggestions.

★ Talk about the wind and introduce new vocabulary to the children, such as 'howl', 'gale' and 'breeze'.

★ Encourage the children to tell a windy-day story using their own words and pictures they have drawn to help them.

## Mathematical development

★ Make a milkshake (perhaps for the party). Measure the milk, ice-cream and syrup flavouring and whisk together. If you are using a clear bowl, look at the milkshake from the outside to see how much froth there is compared to liquid.

★ Put together a simple questionnaire with tick boxes to find out how many children are wearing trousers, skirts, T-shirts, jumpers and so on. The ticks can then be counted and made into a simple block graph or towers of Unifix cubes.

## Knowledge and understanding of the world

★ Make a display of clothing and equipment needed for different sports activities. Ask the children to contribute items for the display from home. Label the display and read the words with the children.

★ Invite the children to think about why we have different clothes for different activities and different weather. Focus on the properties of different materials, such as the thickness of a woollen jumper or the stretchiness of a swimming costume.

## Physical development

★ Pretend to be out walking in different kinds of weather. Encourage the children to jump and splash through the puddles on a rainy day, to battle against the wind holding on to their hats on a windy day, to make and throw snowballs on a snowy day and so on.

★ Provide two adult-size pairs of dungarees and let the children race to put them on.

## Creative development

★ Design a fancy-dress outfit using collage materials. Talk about the character you are designing and the features you could add, such as an eyepatch for a pirate.

*Early years wishing well: Clothes and food*

# Food for the barbecue

Here's our barbecue,
Sizzling hot,
Let's have a look,
To see what we've got.
Pieces of chicken,
Burgers, too.
Lots and lots of sausages,
Sausages, sausages.
I love sausages.
How about you?

Jan Pollard

*Early years wishing well: Clothes and food*

# Food for the barbecue

## Personal, social and emotional development

★ Find out if any of the children have been to a barbecue. Was it to mark a special occasion? Was it a family celebration? Talk about how special occasions and festivals are often centred around food.

★ Consider with the children the dangers of barbecues and what types of safety precautions are needed. Long cooking tools, aprons, gloves and keeping away from the fire could all be discussed.

## Communication, language and literacy

★ Make a list of food that could be cooked on a barbecue. Incorporate the words into a simple story about a barbecue that includes who was present and what the people ate.

★ Create a role-play barbecue area and encourage the children to draw upon your discussions in their play.

## Mathematical development

★ Make a bar chart showing the children's favourite barbecue foods. The children could draw the sausages, veggie burgers and so on along the bottom of the chart and then each child could fill in their name in a box in their chosen column.

★ Imagine you are going to buy food for a barbecue and write a shopping list, counting how many of each item you will need so that there is enough for everyone. Keep the list simple, perhaps bread rolls, burgers and cans of soft drink.

## Knowledge and understanding of the world

★ Use a disposable barbecue in your outdoor area to cook a selection of barbecue food. Let the children watch from a safe distance and ensure that no children approach the barbecue even after cooking. Talk about how the coals remain hot for a long time after the fire has gone out. Once the food has cooled down, let the children sample them and discuss their taste.

★ Discuss why barbecues take place outside. Talk about open fires inside and the need for a chimney to take the smoke away.

## Physical development

★ Use construction toys or large bricks to build a barbecue in the role-play area.

★ Encourage the development of the children's hand–eye co-ordination by inviting them to use food tongs to serve food when they are playing at their barbecue.

## Creative development

★ Let the children draw with charcoal on white paper. Show them how to blend the black lines with their fingers. Use the charcoal to make rubbings of rough surfaces or tyres.

★ Sing 'Ten Fat Sausages Sizzling in a Pan', in *This Little Puffin…* compiled by Elizabeth Matterson (Puffin Books), using your fingers to represent the sausages.

# Lunch box

Lunch boxes,
Munch boxes,
Pink, blue, red!
*I've* got cheese and apple
and thirteen loaves of bread!

Lunch boxes,
Munch boxes,
Yellow, white, blue!
*I've* got twenty sandwiches,
How about you?

Lunch boxes,
Munch boxes,
Brown, black, pink!
*Mine* is full of jelly beans
(At least, that's what I *think!*)

Lunch boxes,
Munch boxes,
Purple, orange, green!
*Mine* is full of chocolate drops
and strawberry ice-cream!

Lunch boxes,
Munch boxes,
Scarlet, emerald, grey!
*Mine's* a finger-licking secret...
What's in *yours* today?

Judith Nicholls

**Early years wishing well: Clothes and food**

# Lunch box

## Personal, social and emotional development

★ Play the 'Lunch box game' with groups of four children. Copy the photocopiable sheets on pages 88 and 89. Cut out the spinner on page 89 and attach the arrow with a split-pin fastener. Laminate page 88 and cut out the cards. Provide each child with a white piece of paper divided into four and explain that this is their lunch box. Let the children take it in turns to spin the spinner and choose an item from the category that the arrow lands on to put into their lunch box. If the arrow lands on a category they already have an item for, they miss a turn. The first child to fill all four sections of their lunch box wins.

## Communication, language and literacy

★ Write out the words 'lunch' and 'munch' onto a piece of card. Cut off the last two letters and talk about 'c' and 'h' together making the 'ch' sound. As a group, try to think of other words that end with this sound – for example, 'crunch' and 'punch'. Older children may be able to suggest how to write these words.

## Mathematical development

★ Make sandwiches with the children and cut them into squares, rectangles and triangles. Talk about cutting these into halves or quarters and let the children advise you as to how to do this. Discuss fitting the pieces back together to make a whole and invite the children to try this themselves.

★ Give the children a bag of jelly beans and ask them to sort them by colour. Count how many there are of each colour and how many there are altogether. Give the children a jelly bean each to eat. Ask the children if there are more or less now and see if they can tell you how many less.

## Knowledge and understanding of the world

★ Talk about foods you might have in your lunch box. Discuss what would have happened to the strawberry ice-cream in the rhyme if it had been left in a lunch box.

★ Look at the different ways of keeping food cool. Leave a tray of frozen ice by a radiator so that the children can observe it turning to water. Ask them what has happened to the ice. How could they make the water turn solid again?

## Physical development

★ Make a collection of boxes or tins with lids on. Encourage the children to match the lids to the boxes and to take them on and off to develop manipulation and control.

## Creative development

★ Allow the children to design and make their own lunch boxes using a selection of old packaging. Talk about different ways to make a lid that opens and stays shut.

# Family food sense

Daddy likes pickled onions
He says they *smell* of spice.

Mummy likes boxed chocolates
She says they *look* so nice.

My brother likes to *hear* the sizzle
Of bacon in the pan.

My baby sister likes the *feel*
Of gooey sticky jam!

But me, I like my fish and chips
They *smell* and *taste* so good.

I'd like to have them everyday
If only that I could!

Brenda Williams

# Family food sense

## Personal, social and emotional development

★ Talk about the children's favourite foods and those of members of their families. Discuss why they like certain foods.

★ Put a variety of foods, herbs or spices into separate containers with thin material secured to the top. Ask the children to guess what is inside the containers by smelling or shaking them. Curry powder, lemon, cornflakes and rice are all good for this.

## Communication, language and literacy

★ Encourage each child to make a family food book. Ask them to draw pictures of members of their families eating their favourite foods. Scribe for the children captions to accompany each picture and join the pictures to make a book.

## Mathematical development

★ Invite the children to count how many people are mentioned in the poem. Can each child tell you if there are more or less people in their family than in the poem?

★ Encourage the children to draw pictures of the members of their families in order of size or age.

★ Provide the children with a tray from an old chocolate selection box and encourage them to make different-shaped chocolates to fit each compartment using Plasticine or play dough.

## Knowledge and understanding of the world

★ Invite a dentist to visit your setting to talk to the children about looking after their teeth and the different foods that are good and bad for them.

★ Develop the role-play area into a dentist's surgery and encourage the children to recall what the dentist has told them.

★ Talk about different types of food and how they are made. Can the children name foods that are healthy and those they should not eat too much of?

## Physical development

★ Visit the local shops and find out what types of food they sell. Which shops sell just food? Which sell other things as well as food? What types of food do different shops sell?

★ Encourage each child to imagine their favourite meal and mime buying the ingredients for it, preparing it, then eating it.

## Creative development

★ Ask the children to create their favourite meal on a plate using paper and a selection of collage materials. Display the finished plates with captions.

★ Use the illustrated recipe sheet on the photocopiable sheet on page 90 to make salt dough. Create a variety of food that could be used in the role-play area. When the salt dough has dried, encourage the children to paint it in suitable colours.

# Cups and saucers

Cups and saucers
Fat teapot
Hold the handle
Tea is hot!

Big plates, small plates
Round deep bowls
Some for soup and
Some for rolls.

Knife for butter
Fork for peas
Spoon for ice-cream
Mmmmm, yes please!

Clear the dishes
Stack the cups
In the sink to
Wash them up!

Brenda Williams

**Early years wishing well: Clothes and food**

# Cups and saucers

## Personal, social and emotional development

★ Have a party or coffee morning for parents and carers and let the children serve drinks and food to the guests. Encourage them to ask what people would like, remembering to say please and thank you. The children can help to lay the tables, wash up and put away the crockery used.

## Communication, language and literacy

★ Talk about having a party and different ways to invite friends. Ask the children what information would need to be on an invitation. Let them help you to word-process invitations for the coffee morning. Give one to each child to deliver to their parents or carers and encourage them to sign their own name if they are able.

★ Scribe the expression 'Mmmmm' for the children and make the sound with them. Talk about what they think it means and invite them to make other suggestions for sounds we make vocally and what they can mean, such as 'Aaaah' and 'Ooooh'. Scribe the children's suggestions.

## Mathematical development

★ In the role-play area, set a table matching cups and saucers by colour. Look at the shape and size of the saucers and plates. Ask the children if they can find circles on the cups and whether they can see more than one.

★ Make repeating patterns using cups, saucers and plates. The children could continue the pattern or make their own.

## Knowledge and understanding of the world

★ Make bread with the children. Look at the ingredients and talk about where they come from. Let the children smell the yeast. Observe the changes as the dough rises and is cooked. Look at the bubbles or pockets of air in the dough. Talk about the heat changing the consistency of the dough and the colour.

## Physical development

★ Have a cup-and-saucer race with the children using plastic cups and saucers in a similar way to an egg-and-spoon race.

★ Stand plastic cups on upturned buckets and see if the children can knock them off using beanbags or sponge balls.

## Creative development

★ Look at the designs on cups and saucers. They can sometimes have a scene on them or a pattern. Allow each child to design their own pattern on a paper plate or cup.

★ Invite the children to make their own 'china', using clay that does not need firing. Coiling long sausages of clay into bowl shapes is probably the simplest method. Smooth the surface using a damp sponge. Once the pots are dry, encourage the children to paint and varnish them.

**Early years wishing well: Clothes and food**

# Fruit

(Finger action rhyme)

Apples, bananas, cherries and plums,
Here are my fingers and here are my thumbs.

Pineapple, strawberry, orange and pear,
Here are my eyes and here is my hair.

Nectarine, grapes, a peach from the tree,
Here is my elbow and here is my knee.

Grapefruit, melon, date and mango,
Here is my ankle and here is my toe.

Here is my shoulder and here is my chest,
I can't decide which fruit is best!

Fruit is good, so don't you agree?
It helps to make the whole body – that's ME!

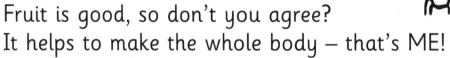

Val Jeans-Jakobsson

# Fruit

## Personal, social and emotional development

★ Invite the children to help you make a person from pieces of fruit. For example, use a pineapple top for hair, bananas for arms and legs, kiwi slices for eyes and so on. Explain to the group that the fruit that you have peeled and touched a lot should not be eaten. Talk about washing hands before touching food that you are going to eat and washing fruit before eating it.

## Communication, language and literacy

★ Make flash cards using pictures of fruit and parts of the body mentioned in the poem. Write the name of the fruit or body part under each picture and laminate the cards. Ask the children to look at the initial letters of all the words. Encourage them to tell you, or tell them, the name and sound of each initial letter. As you say the poem, hold up the flash cards and encourage the children to say the words with you.

## Mathematical development

★ Display a collection of citrus fruit (orange, lemon, tangerine, grapefruit and so on). Ask the children which shape is the odd one out. Talk about spheres and put the fruit spheres in order of size.
★ Take apart the segments in an orange or tangerine and invite the children to count them with you.

## Knowledge and understanding of the world

★ Talk about the seeds and pips found in fruit. Look at different types of fruit and ask the children to guess whether they will have seeds or pips inside them. Allow the children to look closely at the seeds and pips using magnifying glasses.
★ Take the stone from an avocado pear. Insert cocktail sticks firmly into each end. Balance these over a glass containing water. The stone will split and send out a root and a shoot, which can then be planted.

## Physical development

★ Play a traditional game of 'Apple bobbing'. Place a small apple in a bowl of cold water. Ask for volunteers to try and pick the apple up from the bowl using just their mouths. Change the water and use a fresh apple for each child.
★ Visit a 'pick-your-own' fruit farm during the summer. Let the children pick some fruit, such as strawberries, reminding them to be careful not to damage them. Wash and enjoy!

## Creative development

★ Use under-ripe fruit to make prints (for example, apples and pears. Cut them in half and dip them into paint or printing inks. Use fruit-shaped paper for the children to print on.
★ Make musical instruments. Put seeds, fruit stones and pips in bags, tubs or boxes. Investigate the difference in sound when seeds are in a cloth bag and a plastic box.

*Early years wishing well: Clothes and food*

# Delicious dishes

Poppadum, dhal, chapatti, curry:
Indian food's too good to hurry.

Bean sprouts, noodles, soy sauce, rice:
Chinese food is also nice.

Pizza, breadsticks, pasta and sauce:
Italian food is great, of course.

Go north or south or west or east
In many a place you'll find a feast.

Go north or south or east or west
To find which foods you like the best.

Tony Mitton

**Early years wishing well: Clothes and food**

# Delicious dishes

## Personal, social and emotional development

★ Talk with the children about the foods eaten in other countries and the smells that you might notice when you pass an Indian or Chinese take-away.

★ Ask the children if they have ever visited another country, if they ate any unusual foods there and if they enjoyed them.

## Communication, language and literacy

★ Introduce the children to a few simple words in another language.

★ Change the role-play area into an Indian, Chinese or Italian restaurant. Help the children to write an appropriate menu on a large sheet of paper and encourage them to use the words in their play.

★ Let the children paint pictures of their favourite food and help them to label them.

## Mathematical development

★ Use coins from other countries and talk to the group about how we pay for food in shops. Do the children recognize any of the numbers on the coins?

★ Use the coins in a café role-play area to pay for food and give as change.

★ Make two copies of the photocopiable sheet on page 91, laminate them and cut the cards out. Let the children use them to play 'Pairs'. Then talk about where the different foods come from.

## Knowledge and understanding of the world

★ Show the children a compass. Explain to them that explorers use compasses to find the direction they want to go in. Talk to the children about the sun coming up in the east and setting in the west. Go outside and show the children the direction of east and west. Repeat this so that the children realize that the sun always comes up in the same place and sets in the same place.

## Physical development

★ Mark the walls or edges of a large space with the letters N (north), S (south), E (east) and W (west). Place four large hoops on the floor by the letters, each with enough items of food packaging in them for each child playing the game. Ask the children to stand in the middle of the space and explain that when you say 'go' you would like them to run to one of the hoops, pick up an item of food and return to the centre. When everyone has collected their food, they should tell you which direction they went in to get it.

## Creative development

★ Using plain pizza bases and a variety of toppings such as cheese, ham, pepperoni, pineapple, tomatoes, peppers and mushrooms, encourage the children to create their own pizzas, providing help where necessary. Bake the pizzas and eat them at snack time.

# Mr Bobby's sweet stall

Every Saturday, Kevin and Katie went to the big Market Hall in town with their mum. Their favourite place was Mr Bobby's sweet stall. It was packed full of every kind of sweets and chocolates you could think of.

Mr Bobby was very kind. He always made sure that there was something every young customer could buy, even if they didn't have much pocket money. His sweet stall had been in the market for as long as anyone could remember.

'I used to buy *my* Saturday sweets from Mr Bobby,' said their mum.

One Saturday, the shutters on Mr Bobby's stall were pulled down. No Mr Bobby!

'That's strange,' said their mum. 'I didn't know Mr Bobby was going on holiday. He always puts up a notice.'

The next Saturday it was the same.

Katie and Kevin were very disappointed.

'Something is wrong,' said their mum. 'Let's go and ask Mrs Brown on the egg stall.'

'The poor man's in hospital,' Mrs Brown told them. 'He's had an operation and isn't at all well. And him all alone, too.'

'Right,' said their mum. 'Let's go and choose a nice get-well card and some flowers, and I'll take them round to the hospital for Mr Bobby.'

'How was Mr Bobby, Mum?' asked Kevin and Katie when their mum got back from the hospital.

'He was ever so pleased with the card and flowers,' she told them, 'but he looked very tired. He was thinking about retiring. Giving up the stall.'

'Oh, no! He can't do that!' said Kevin.

'Tell him...' said Katie, '...tell him he's got to come back because we've got a special surprise for him.'

'Have we?' said Kevin, puzzled.

'Yes,' said Katie. 'I've just thought of it. But we'll need to get everyone who knows Mr Bobby to help.'

'That's loads of people!' said Kevin.

'We'll have to get started, then!' said Katie.

When Mr Bobby came back to the market, he couldn't believe his eyes. There was a big crowd round his stall. There were banners, balloons, ribbons, cards and posters all over it, saying things like 'Welcome Back!' 'Lots of Love!' 'We've Missed you!'. Kevin and Katie, and all Mr Bobby's friends had made them.

'Well!' said Mr Bobby, blowing his nose in a large hanky, 'it looks as if I shall have to put off retiring for a bit!'

'YES!' shouted everyone.

Patricia Leighton

**Early years wishing well: Clothes and food**

# Mr Bobby's sweet stall

## Personal, social and emotional development

★ Kevin and Katie were very kind to Mr Bobby. Ask the children if someone has ever been kind to them and what they did. Discuss different ways to make someone feel special.

★ Talk about hospitals with the children. Explain that if you are badly hurt or very ill, you can go there to be made better. Ask the children if any of them have ever been to a hospital and encourage them to share their experiences.

## Communication, language and literacy

★ Change the role-play area into a hospital with forms on clipboards and appointment books for the children to fill out.

★ Cut banner shapes out of large pieces of paper and let the children write their names or messages on them in bright colours.

## Mathematical development

★ Sort beads by colour into large sweet jars and display them in a row with a set of balance scales and some small baskets. Encourage the children to select beads in their baskets as though they were choosing a 'pick-and-mix' and then weigh them on the scales. Younger children could just weigh their sweets against an item, such as a book, to see if they are heavier or lighter.

★ Bring in a bag of sweets and use them to do simple addition and subtraction. At the end of the session, count out the sweets, then give one to each child and count how many are left over. Can they be shared out equally?

## Knowledge and understanding of the world

★ Visit a market to see what sort of stalls there are. Make comparisons between open-air markets and big supermarkets.

★ Name the days of the week and talk about the difference between Saturdays and Sundays and the rest of the days.

## Physical development

★ Have a race to see who can be the first to unscrew the lid of a jar of sweets (or bead 'sweets') take out three sweets one by one and screw the lid back on. Play the game again with different containers.

★ Provide a selection of wrapping paper and parcel decorations for the children to wrap gifts. Encourage them to practise using scissors and sticky-tape dispensers as they wrap and tie their parcels.

## Creative development

★ Give the children a variety of sweet-wrappers and chocolate-wrappers to make a large collage of a sweet.

★ Make peppermint creams with the children and put them into decorated boxes for the children to take home as presents for their parents or carers. Some of the sweets could be coloured with food colouring.

# Food, glorious food!

May Lee was looking forward to school today. They were going to do some more cooking.

Last time, Sarah's mum had come to school and they had made fairy cakes. They watched through the window of the microwave oven as the sticky mixture of flour, margarine, eggs, sugar and milk grew into light little cakes in their paper cases. May Lee had put icing and a red sweet on hers.

One week they had made chapattis with Jaspreet's mum. They stirred the brown flour, salt and water together to make a ball of dough. Then they each took a small piece, made it into a ball and rolled it flat with a rolling-pin into a circle shape. The chapattis were cooked on the stove, in a flat iron pan with a long handle. May Lee's chapatti was a funny shape and had a few holes in it, but when Mrs Atwal plopped a spoonful of jam on it, May Lee found it tasted delicious.

When Devon's dad came to school, they made Johnny cakes with flour, salt and water – just like chapattis, only the flour was white this time. Mr Giles dropped their balls of dough very carefully into a pan of deep, hot oil. They bubbled and sizzled as they cooked. When the cakes were cool enough, they took them back to the classroom to eat.

But today was very special for May Lee. Her grandad had come to show them how to cook in a wok.

First, they cut up an onion and some garlic. Then they grated a piece of knobbly ginger root. Next they cut up some Chinese leaves, which looked like a long, pointy lettuce.

Mr Lee quickly fried the ginger, garlic and onion in the wok with some sugar and salt.

He tossed in the Chinese leaves with a spoon of wine vinegar and stirred everything round. It smelled wonderful.

Mr Lee served everyone with some of the stir-fry in small bowls. Then he gave them chopsticks to use. They all looked at them with dismay! Even their teacher wasn't very good at using them, and there was a great deal of shrieking and laughter as they tried to pick up their food. Those sticks just wouldn't do as they were told!

May Lee was the only one who could eat the Chinese leaves with chopsticks. The other children thought she was very clever, but May Lee and her grandad just smiled happily as the rest of them used spoons.

> **Glossary**
> *Chapattis: flat bread made with wholemeal flour (attah) and water, cooked on a griddle. Made daily to accompany – or scoop up – Indian dishes.*
> *Johnny cakes: tasty little deep-fried dumplings. 'Johnny' is a corruption of 'journey' – these cakes would be very sustaining for a hungry traveller! The dumplings are Caribbean (Jamaican) in origin.*

Barbara Moore

**Early years wishing well: Clothes and food**

# Food, glorious food!

## Personal, social and emotional development

★ If any of the children's parents or carers originate from different cultures, invite them to your setting to talk about their traditional food, how it is cooked and the tools that they use for cooking and eating. They could also make the food and let the children sample it.

★ Make a display of Chinese cooking tools, dry ingredients, chopsticks, rice bowls and teapots and cups for the children to look at and handle. Write labels for the items on display in Chinese and English.

## Communication, language and literacy

★ Introduce the children to Chinese writing. Talk about the characters being written from top to bottom rather than left to right as in English. Provide large versions of some of the simpler Chinese characters for the children to try and copy onto long strips of paper using paint and brushes.

★ Look at information books on China and make comparisons between life there and here.

## Mathematical development

★ Make a collection of food packages. Look at their sizes, shapes and weights.

★ Make a shop in your role-play area using the packages from the previous activity. Cut the food names from the labels of matching packaging and attach these to shelves so that the children can identify where to put packages when they tidy up. Encourage them to count the packages back onto the shelves.

★ The packages from the previous activities could be grouped into sets either by size or content – for example, all the large packages or all the cereal packages could be put together as they are in a supermarket.

## Knowledge and understanding of the world

★ Grow some beans to use in a salad or in cooking. Put bean seeds in a jar, fill the jar with water and then empty it out. Cover the jar with muslin or fine cloth. Put the jar in a cupboard. Each day for four days, you will need to fill the jar with water and empty it out. By the fifth day, the sprouts should have appeared and be ready to use.

## Physical development

★ Allow the children to try using chopsticks or rice bowls and spoons for eating.

★ Put a selection of Chinese clothing in the role-play area so that the children can practise dressing and undressing.

## Creative development

★ Invite the children to make kites or Chinese lanterns, using the traditional gold and red Chinese colours.

★ Play some Chinese music and allow the children to move to the music or use a long piece of material to re-enact the Chinese dragon dance.

# The best vegetable

The vegetables in the vegetable patch were arguing over which vegetable was the best.

'Potatoes are the best, of course,' boasted a potato. 'Potatoes are so useful. They can be chipped, mashed, roasted, baked and made into crisps. Everyone loves potatoes.'

'Rubbish!' scoffed a carrot. 'Potatoes are boring. Not like carrots. For a start, carrots are orange, such a bright, pretty colour! And they're full of goodness. Carrots can be eaten raw, boiled, chopped up and popped into stews and soups or grated for salads. Carrots are definitely the best vegetable.'

'Hmph!' snorted the spinach. 'Spinach is much better than potatoes or carrots. Its dark green leaves are rich in iron and are healthy to eat.'

'Cabbage leaves are green too,' piped up the cabbage. 'And cabbage is much tastier than spinach.'

'Not as a tasty as cauliflower,' boasted a cauliflower. 'Everyone loves cauliflower cooked in cheese sauce. It is even served in the top restaurants.'

The onions bristled crossly. 'Onions are far more useful,' snapped an onion. 'Onions are sliced and fried for hot dogs, chopped up for salads or added to soups, curries and stews. Onions are definitely the best vegetable.'

As the other vegetables argued around them, the tiny peas slept in their pods and said nothing.

The vegetables argued all morning. They were still arguing when a little girl skipped down the path towards the vegetable patch.

'Right, we'll soon sort out this argument,' decided the potato. 'Whichever vegetable this little girl picks first is the best.'

The vegetables all waited with bated breath as the little girl reached the vegetable patch and looked around. She walked past the rows of potatoes, carrots, cabbages, cauliflowers and onions, then stopped by the tall thin canes where the peas were growing. Smiling, she picked a pea pod, opened it and popped the peas, one by one into her mouth. Then she turned around and skipped back up the garden path.

'See, peas are the best!' chanted the other peas. 'Peas don't need cooking or washing, they can be eaten straight from the pod!'

Then the peas nestled down in their pods and went to sleep again. And as for all the other vegetables, they were too astonished to argue any more!

Karen King

**Early years wishing well: Clothes and food**

# The best vegetable

## Personal, social and emotional development

★ In the story, all the vegetables thought they were the best. Discuss how it is good to be proud of ourselves but explain that boasting can make us seem like we do not appreciate other people enough.

★ The vegetables were unhappy when the little girl did not pick them. Talk about how it feels to be left out of games. Encourage the children to think about how their actions can affect others.

## Communication, language and literacy

★ Make the role-play area into a garden centre with packets of seeds and small vegetable plants. Encourage the children to take on different roles and to use the appropriate language for the role. Observe their play and prompt them where necessary.

★ Make a copy of the photocopiable sheet on page 92 for each child. Cut out the pictures and ask the children to colour them in and then sequence the story of going to buy some vegetables at the market.

## Mathematical development

★ Make a number line to ten using the children's paintings of vegetables – 1 onion, 2 carrots, 3 potatoes and so on.

★ Buy some peas in pods and give one each to a small group of children. Ask each child to open them carefully so that they do not loose any of the peas, and to count how many there are in the pod. How many pods have the same number of peas in them? Who has the most peas in their pod? And the least?

## Knowledge and understanding of the world

★ Grow peas or beans in clear containers. Put some rolled-up kitchen paper inside an old jam jar so that it rests against the sides, slide pea or bean seeds between the paper and the container, ensuring that they do not go down to the bottom. Add a small quantity of water so that the paper is moist. Put the container on a warm window sill and keep it moist. Watch the roots and then the shoots form.

★ Grow cress on cotton wool in eggshells with faces on. The cress will grow to look like hair.

## Physical development

★ During a movement session, ask the children to pretend to be little seeds growing into plants. Invite them to express growth with their movements.

## Creative development

★ Make vegetables for the role-play area from salt dough (see the recipe on the photocopiable sheet on page 90). Bake them, allow them to cool, then paint and varnish them.

★ Read the children the story of 'The Enormous Turnip' (traditional) and let them re-create the story, taking on the roles of the different characters.

# Go bananas!

Bananas are sweet and soft, and easy to eat. Did you know that marathon runners, tennis players and bike riders will often have a few bites of bananas to keep them going?

Bananas grow in hot countries. Banana trees have thick trunks and big, wide leaves. Red flowers grow out of the middle of the trunk. When the flower opens up, the centre starts to grow a stem of bananas. It takes a long time for the bananas to grow big enough to eat, but each stem can have as many as one hundred bananas on it!

In one country, they put blue bags round the stem of the bananas, to keep them safe from the weather and pests.

Bananas get ripe very quickly. Because they have to go on very long journeys, they have to be picked when they are still hard and green. Then they are packed into big, refrigerator ships that take them all over the world. Once they arrive in this country, they are put into a warm, damp room to ripen slowly. When they are nearly ripe, they are cut into bunches – called 'hands' – and sent out to the fruit shops and supermarkets.

Have a good look at the bananas next time you go shopping. If the skins are going spotty and brown, they are too ripe. If they are green they are not ripe enough. But if they are yellow, they are just right for you to eat!

There are many ways to eat bananas, too. A Banana Split is made with a banana cut right down the middle, to make a boat shape. Then it is filled with fruit (strawberries, cherries, or whatever is your favourite) and finally a scoop of ice-cream is put at each end. Some people like to put a dollop of whipped cream on as well. Yum!

Patricia Leighton

**Early years wishing well: Clothes and food**

# Go bananas!

## Personal, social and emotional development

★ Invite the children to think about why the marathon runners, tennis players and bike riders need a few bites of banana to keep them going. Discuss how food gives us energy. Talk about not eating too much or too little before exercising, to ensure that we don't get indigestion but that we have enough energy.

## Communication, language and literacy

★ Discuss with the children the sequence of events in a banana's life, from the flower forming on the banana tree to its arrival in a supermarket. Ask the children to make story cards to sequence the journey, with each child drawing a different stage.

## Mathematical development

★ Take the group to a local park to look at the thicknesses of tree trunks. Ask the children to show you a tree that has a thick trunk and another that has a thin trunk. With the children's help, put a piece of string around the thickest tree trunk and cut it to the width of the tree trunk. See if any other trees have trunks the same width using the string as a measure.

★ Give each child a copy of the photocopiable sheet on page 93. Ask them to count the bananas in each 'hand' and record the number in the box.

★ Ask the children to carry out a survey of favourite fruit in the group and make a block graph of your results.

## Knowledge and understanding of the world

★ Take the children to a local shop to buy some under-ripe bananas. Ask the children what colour under-ripe bananas are. Take the bananas back to your setting and record in pictures and words the changes that the children see as the bananas ripen. You could put the over-ripe banana outside to watch it decompose.

★ Think of some other ways to eat bananas, such as banana bread and banana smoothies.

## Physical development

★ Take a variety of small soft balls and bats outside. Challenge the children to see if they can hit the ball up in the air as if they are tennis players. Perhaps they can hit it a few times before it touches the floor. Encourage them to count how many times they can hit the ball.

## Creative development

★ Make a collection of wide leaves. Ask the children to paint on the veined side of the leaf and then press a piece of plain paper onto it to make a print. When the leaves are dry, cut them out and attach them to kitchen-roll tubes that have been painted like trunks, to make banana trees.

# Fish fingers

Mmm, fish fingers! Scrumptious sticks of fish in crispy, golden crumbs.

Of course, fish don't have fingers! Have you ever thought about how they are made?

First, the fishermen have to catch the fish in their nets and bring them ashore. Then the fish are cut up. The parts that are going to be made into fish fingers are carefully cleaned. No one wants bones in these fingers!

At the factory, the fish pieces are pressed together into big blocks and frozen solid. The blocks move along to the next machine that cuts them into the small 'fingers' or sticks.

Then the fingers pass through a runny mixture of flour, starch, water and salt. This makes them nice and sticky.

Next, they go to the crumbing machine. Here they are shaken about until every bit of them is covered in lovely, yummy crumbs. The crumbs are soft, though, so the fish fingers have to be dipped quickly in a big pan of boiling fat. This makes the crumb coating go hard, but it doesn't cook the fish.

The fish fingers are lifted out of the pan and frozen again. Then another machine packs them into their bright cardboard boxes.

Special refrigerated lorries have to be used to take them to the shops and supermarkets all over the country. We have to keep them in the freezer at home, too, so that they stay fresh until we are ready to cook them.

Patricia Leighton

# Fish fingers

## Personal, social and emotional development

★ Talk about the people who work to bring us food – the farmers, fishermen, bakers and so on. Ask if any of the children's families grow or make food and, if so, what they do.

★ Fishermen are often at sea for a long time. Discuss with the children what it would be like not to see members of their families for a long time.

## Communication, language and literacy

★ Prepare a collection of empty frozen food packages. Ask the children what they think was in the packages and why they think that – it will probably be from looking at the pictures! Point out the names of the foods on the packages for the children.

★ Encourage each child to design their own fish-finger packaging. Invite them to write the name of the product on the box, providing help if necessary.

## Mathematical development

★ Use the plastic fish fingers from the home corner, or make some from play dough. Count them as you put them in a box. Take out one or two and ask the children how many are in the box now. Repeat this, removing different numbers of fish fingers each time and asking the children whether there are more or less in the box or out of it, counting with them if necessary.

★ Look at the heating instructions on a packet of fish fingers. Cook some at your setting and ask the children to help you set the timer and the oven correctly.

## Knowledge and understanding of the world

★ Look at information books about fish and find out how they breathe under water and how they use their tails to swim.

★ If you have a fish tank, let the children observe the way that fish move in water, opening and closing their mouths and gills.

## Physical development

★ Give each child a copy of the photocopiable sheet on page 94. Invite them to colour in and cut out both fish shapes, and laminate them yourself. Ask the children to place a paper clip on the head of each fish shape. Tie magnets onto string and then onto pieces of dowelling (the children could cut the dowelling using a small hand saw). Put the fish in a bowl and use the magnets as fishing rods to catch them.

## Creative development

★ Invite the children to use construction toys to create a fish-finger factory. Encourage them to retell the story of a fish finger in their own way, using the props they have made. Toy lorries and a road map could also be used to re-create the fish finger's journey to the supermarket.

*Early years wishing well: Clothes and food*

# Sam's birthday party

It would soon be time for Sam's birthday. His mum asked him what kind of cake he wanted this time. Last year he had a tiger-shaped cake, to look like his favourite toy, with stripes made out of marzipan and chocolate.

Sam thought hard. Next to his Tiger, he loved trains and engines best. So he asked his mum if this year he could have a chocolate cake shaped like an engine! Mum thought it was a great idea.

When they went shopping that week, they bought two large chocolate rolls.

Sam put the first roll on the cake board. This would be the front part of the engine. His mum cut four slices from the second roll to make the wheels. Then she trimmed the rest of the roll to make the driver's cab. They stuck the pieces together with icing. Last of all, Sam used some jelly sweets to put a face on the front of the engine. It looked great!

Next day, Sam helped get the food ready for his party. He put some small sausages into a dish to cook them, and when they were done, he stuck some little wooden sticks into each one, to make them easy to pick up.

Then he and Mum made shape sticks: they took some more of the wooden sticks and onto each one pushed a cube of pineapple, a round grape, and a cube of cheese.

Sam wanted some strawberry-jam sandwiches, too. Mum made them just how he liked them and she also made ham sandwiches and tuna sandwiches, as well. They put them onto large plates. There were a few jam sandwiches left over, so Sam used biscuit cutters to cut out large and small circles from each of them.

It was time to set the table. Sam and his mum covered it first with a colourful, party table-cloth. Then they put out paper plates, paper napkins and paper cups – all in the same pattern as the cloth. The rest of the table they filled with the plates of food, bowls of crisps and a dish of small, iced biscuits.

But there was a space left right in the very middle.

What had they forgotten?

Sam's wonderful birthday cake!

Sam just had time to put on the candles before his friends arrived for the party.

How many candles do you think there were?

Brenda Williams

Early years wishing well: Clothes and food

# Sam's birthday party

## Personal, social and emotional development

★ Discuss birthdays and how they are special. Encourage the children to tell you how they celebrate their own birthdays and to talk about the favourite gifts that they have received. Explain to the group that, sometimes, small gift bags are given to the children at birthday parties to say thank you for coming. Talk about how it is nice to give presents as well as to receive them.

## Communication, language and literacy

★ Make birthday cards by writing 'Happy birthday' on the front of folded pieces of A4 card and messages inside. The writing inside the card could be done on a computer. Encourage the children to look at the letter shapes. Ask them to tell you some of the sounds of the letters. Give the cards to the children when it is their birthdays.

## Mathematical development

★ Buy a selection of birthday cards featuring the numbers 1 to 10 and make a number line with them. Use the line to talk about which number comes before or after a given number and to compare numbers, seeing whether they are more or less than one another. Take one of the cards away and ask the children which number is missing. For older children, mix the cards up before asking which number is missing.

## Knowledge and understanding of the world

★ Use an old pan over a low heat to melt down some ends of old candles to make new ones. Put a length of string into a yoghurt carton securing it to the base to form the wick. It should be long enough to reach the top of the carton. Cool the wax and then pour it in. Remove the carton when the wax has set. To make striped candles, add a different-coloured layer when each previous layer has set.

## Physical development

★ Play 'Musical chairs'. Line chairs up in a large space so that they are alternately facing in opposite directions. Ask each child to sit on a chair. Tell them that you are going to play some music and that they are to walk carefully around the chairs. When the music stops, they should go and sit on a chair without pushing or running. When the music starts, take away one chair so that there are not enough chairs for all the children. The child to get the last chair when all the others have been removed wins the game.

## Creative development

★ Using ready-made marzipan and roll-out icing, design the top for a birthday cake. The marzipan and icing can be moulded into shapes, or rolled out with shapes cut from it. Use food colouring to colour the icing and marzipan, or paint with the colouring.

# Picnic surprises!

(Tune: 'Oats and Beans')

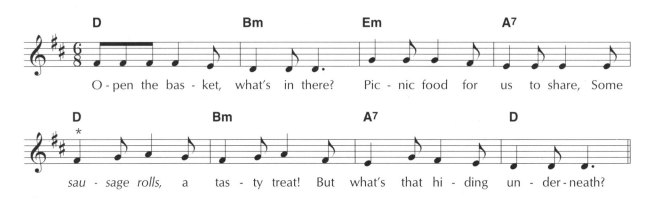

O - pen the bas - ket, what's in there? Pic - nic food for us to share, Some

sau - sage rolls, a tas - ty treat! But what's that hi - ding un - der - neath?

> For extra verses, change the food item.

Sue Nicholls

**Early years wishing well: Clothes and food**

# Picnic surprises!

## Personal, social and emotional development

★ Talk about having a surprise. Discuss how some surprises are pleasant and how others can be unpleasant. Ask the children if they have had an unpleasant surprise such as property being damaged or lost, or finding that they have forgotten something.

★ Talk about different types of food that can be taken on picnics and decide which are healthy and which are less healthy.

## Communication, language and literacy

★ Make copies for each child (or pairs of children) of the photocopiable sheets on pages 95 and 96. Ask them to cut out the food that would be suitable to take on a picnic and glue them onto the basket and explain that this could be used as a list to check what to take if they were going on a real picnic. Discuss why people write lists.

## Mathematical development

★ Provide picnic foods, such as sandwiches, that the children can share at snack time, ensuring that there will be enough for each child to have two or three. Count how many sandwiches there are and how many children to share them. Ask the children to guess how many they will get each. Pass the sandwiches around until they have all gone. Ask the children how many they got each and if it was the same as their guess.

## Knowledge and understanding of the world

★ Discuss the seasons and when you are most likely to go on a picnic.

★ Ask the children if they have ever been on a picnic and what they took with them. Discuss the differences between picnics and other meals. Talk about other occasions when they might eat outside.

★ Food was hidden in the song. Ask the children about other things that might hide. Look under stones to see what creatures are hiding there. Identify some of the creatures you have seen using reference books and make observational drawings of the creatures.

## Physical development

★ Make a collection of travel rugs, plates, cups, bags or baskets and packed picnic foods for the children to organize a picnic. Go outside and encourage the children to pretend to climb hills, push through branches in a wood, balance as they cross a narrow bridge and use different movements to get to the picnic area, where you can enjoy your hard-earned meal!

## Creative development

★ Surprise the children by mixing paint. Put blobs of paint on cellophane, fold it in half and press the cellophane to mix the paint together. Put paper on top of the unfolded cellophane and press to form a print. Talk about which colours have mixed together and the new colour that they have made.

**Early years wishing well: Clothes and food**

# What's outside the food?

*Steadily*

| D | D7 | G | Em | A7 | | D | A7 | D |

Crisps in pack-ets made of foil, Plas-tic bot-tles full of cook-ing oil.

| | D7 | G | Em | A7 | | D | A7 | D |

Cakes in card-board box-es, stack them up! Fiz-zy drink in a pret-ty pa-per cup!

> *Use the packaging material mentioned in the song to provide sounds to accompany the song, for example, crumple foil, run a stick along a grooved plastic bottle, play cardboard boxes like drums and make a paper cup into a shaker using pasta and a cling-film lid. Make a collection of packaging materials. How many will produce sounds?*

Sue Nicholls

**Early years wishing well: Clothes and food**

# What's outside the food?

## Personal, social and emotional development

★ Take the children for a walk along the street to see if any rubbish has been dropped. Discuss how the street could be tidied. Ask what should happen to food wrappings such as crisp packets when they are finished with. Encourage older children to design posters to remind others to put their rubbish in the bins provided in the street or keep them till they get home.

## Communication, language and literacy

★ Talk about why we need packaging for food. Scribe the children's ideas on a whiteboard, then encourage the group to help you make lists of types of food that are pre-packed and those that are not.

## Mathematical development

★ Provide a collection of different cylindrical plastic bottles and ask the children to put them in order of height. Then invite them to look at the bottom of the bottles and put them in order of size of diameter. Encourage them to talk about whether the order is the same in both cases.

★ Put a collection of bottles in the water tray. Discuss whether they are full or empty and how many small bottles of water will fill larger bottles. Encourage the children to experiment with the bottles to check whether their guesses were correct.

## Knowledge and understanding of the world

★ Peel some potatoes to make crisps with. Slice them thinly and put them in cold water for a few minutes to let some of the starch soak out. Ask the children to look at the colour of the water – it will have gone cloudy because of the starch. Dry the slices well and deep-fry them for 3–4 minutes in a deep fat fryer. (Ensure the children remain at a safe distance). Talk about how manufacturers make crisps this way but on a large scale with big machines.

## Physical development

★ Invite the children to build small wooden blocks as high as they can to make towers. See how high they can build their towers before they fall down.

★ Use Mecanno to make packaging for cakes or a container to carry milk bottles so that they do not break. The use of the screwdrivers and bolts will help the development of the children's manipulative skills.

## Creative development

★ Record a selection of sounds made by some packaging materials, such as the bursting of a crisp packet or the fizz that occurs when you open a bottle of fizzy soft drink. Ask the children to guess what the sounds are and encourage them to make suggestion about other sounds that can be made using packaging.

# Jelly

*With a bit of a wobble*

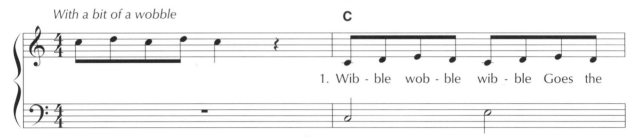

1. Wib - ble wob - ble wib - ble Goes the

jel - ly on the plate. It's jel - ly for tea So don't be late.

2. Sizzle sizzle sizzle
Goes the sausage in the pan
It's sausage for tea
Come as quickly as you can.

> *Shake a tambourine or shaker while you sing the words.*

Susan Eames

# Jelly

## Personal, social and emotional development

★ Talk about why we should try not to be late for events or appointments such as seeing the doctor. Discuss what happens if we make other people wait too long. Think of some reasons for being late. Sometimes there is nothing we can do about it, when the bus is late, for example, but other times we may just need to do things more quickly or get things ready in advance.

## Communication, language and literacy

★ Talk about what the children have for their tea. Ask them to think of words to describe the foods they eat, such as 'sizzling sausages' or 'wobbling jelly'. These suggestions could be made into another verse for the song.

★ When the children are familiar with the song, ask them to point out the words that rhyme. Write these words on a whiteboard with any other rhyming words the children can think of.

## Mathematical development

★ Introduce the children to times of the day and discuss when different meals are eaten. Some of the children may know the times of particular meals. Look at a clock and a digital clock and set them both to appropriate times for breakfast, lunch and tea. Encourage the children to try to name the figures on both clocks.

## Knowledge and understanding of the world

★ Invite the children to make jelly with you. Read the instructions from a jelly packet aloud and ask the children what tools will be required. Prepare the jelly, talking about how it is dissolving or melting. Invite the children to think about why it is safer to use a wooden spoon than a metal spoon when stirring the hot liquid. Pour the jelly into different-shaped moulds and notice how it takes on the shape of the container when it sets. Take the jelly out of the moulds and enjoy it at snack time.

## Physical development

★ Encourage the children to wobble, firstly on the spot, and then as they move around the room.

★ Put the children in small groups and ask them to link together like sausages by holding hands or linking arms and to run sizzling around the room without breaking the link or bumping into one another.

## Creative development

★ Put paper cups, table-cloths, plates, jelly dishes and toy or play-dough sausages into the role-play area, so that the children can re-create making tea, cooking sausages or having a party.

★ Add some water to the sand tray. Provide the children with different moulds and invite them to make different-shaped sand jellies in the wet sand.

# Breakfast's on the table

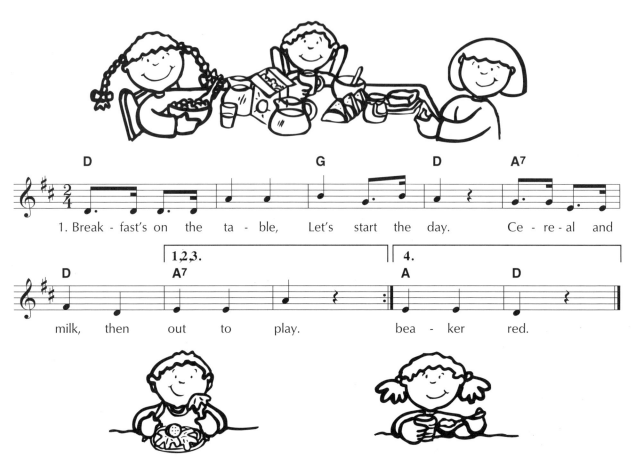

1. Break - fast's on the ta - ble, Let's start the day. Ce - re - al and

milk, then out to play. bea - ker red.

2. Dinner's on the table:
Salad and ham,
Creamy rice pudding with
Strawberry jam.

3. Tea's on the table:
Pizza with cheese,
Crunchy red apple and
Yoghurt, please.

4. Supper's on the table.
Ready for bed?
Warm milky cocoa in my
Beaker red.

Susan Eames

**Early years wishing well: Clothes and food**

# Breakfast's on the table

## Personal, social and emotional development

★ Discuss the children's favourite breakfast cereals and why they like them. Think about everyone liking different things for different reasons and discuss how everyone's opinion is valuable.

## Communication, language and literacy

★ Take a strip of card and fold it into a zigzag of six equal sections. Talk to the children about the food they eat during a day and ask them to record this in their zigzag book. Help the children to think of titles for their books. Ask each child to draw or write the names of their breakfast, dinner, snack and so on from one day, using one page for each meal.

★ Write the words 'breakfast', 'lunch', 'tea' and 'supper' on cards. Mix them up and invite the children to help you put them in the correct order.

## Mathematical development

★ As you sing the song, count how many meals were eaten. Sing the song again to see which foods were eaten first, second and so on. Draw pictures of the foods eaten for the various meals on flash cards. Encourage the children to put them in the order they appear in the song.

★ Draw a large pizza and cut it into eight sections. Ask the children to share it between two, four and then eight.

## Knowledge and understanding of the world

★ Ask if the children have had a hot breakfast and, if so, what they ate. Ask them whether they like eating eggs at breakfast time. If possible, visit a farm with the children to collect fresh eggs. Break open a raw egg into a bowl and show around the yolk, white and shell. Break another egg, putting the shell aside, and mix it up with a fork to look at how it changes. Cook the beaten egg with a little milk and butter to make scrambled eggs or an omelette. Discuss other ways of cooking eggs and, if possible, demonstrate these to the children.

## Physical development

★ Make a circle with the children. Go around the circle telling each child which meal they are: breakfast, lunch, tea and supper (there can be several of each). Call out the name of a meal. The children who are that meal run around the outside of the circle going in one direction without overtaking anyone. When you say, 'Now I'm going to eat you', each child returns to their place, without changing direction. Repeat this so that all the children have a turn.

## Creative development

★ Provide oats, wheat germ, chopped apple and banana, dried fruit and milk. Invite the children to create their own breakfast muesli, which they can then eat at snack time.

# Pop it on a pizza!

(Tune: 'London Bridge is Falling Down')

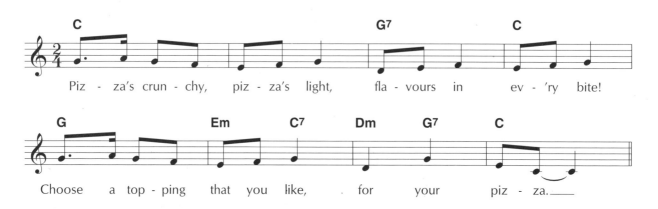

C       G7       C

Piz - za's crun - chy,   piz - za's light,   fla - vours in   ev - 'ry   bite!

G       Em    C7    Dm    G7    C

Choose    a top - ping   that you like,   for   your   piz - za.___

Pass a card disc decorated to look like a pizza around the ring during the verse. Whoever holds the pizza when the song ends chooses a favourite topping. Everyone sings again using the child's name and choice, for example:
'Sally chooses pepper rings,
Pepper rings, pepper rings,
Sally chooses pepper rings,
For her pizza!'

Sue Nicholls

**Early years wishing well: Clothes and food**

# Pop it on a pizza!

## Personal, social and emotional development

★ Discuss how pizza is good food for sharing because it can be cut into slices. Think about other types of food that can be shared easily and why it is good to share food.

## Communication, language and literacy

★ Cut out an apple shape from card. Write 'crunchy' at the top. Ask the children to name foods that are crunchy. Write them onto the card. Repeat the activity for other descriptive words about food.

★ Encourage the children to invent a pizza named after your setting and make a list of all the toppings the group would like to include on it.

## Mathematical development

★ Make a set of dominoes using pictures of pizzas and other foods from magazines and laminate them. Share the dominoes out between groups of four children and invite them to take turns at matching the pictures.

★ Share a pizza in groups of four. Cut the pizza in half and ask the children how many pieces you have made. Encourage them to think about how many pieces you will make if you cut each piece in half again. Talk about the four pieces being quarters. Ask the children what you would need to do to have enough pieces of pizza for them to have two pieces each.

## Knowledge and understanding of the world

★ Pizza is popular in Italy. Look on a globe to find England and Italy and show them to the group. Ask if any of the children have been to Italy. Perhaps they have photographs or postcards from Italy that they could show the rest of the group. Invite the children to tell you about other foods that we enjoy that are traditionally from other countries.

## Physical development

★ Have two or three groups of five children. Cut three large pictures of pizzas into four pieces. Put each pizza and a paper plate on a table at one side of the room. Line the children up in their groups, so that they are playing against the other groups, at the opposite side of the room to the tables. Each team has to collect a plate and the four pizza pieces to make a whole pizza on a plate. Each child can only take one item from the table. Finish by sitting down on the floor.

## Creative development

★ Invite the children to make pizza necklaces using different colours of Fimo. Make balls of Fimo into circular bases and add small pizza topping features. Use a sharp pencil to make a hole in the top of the pendants, then bake them in the oven. When the pizza pendants have cooled, paint them with clear varnish and thread some coloured ribbon through the holes to make necklaces.

# What do you like to eat?

(Tune: 'A Sailor Went to Sea')

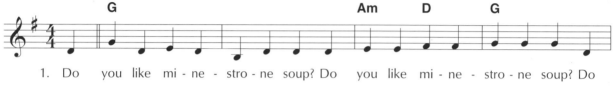

1. Do you like mi-ne-stro-ne soup? Do you like mi-ne-stro-ne soup? Do

you like mi-ne-stro-ne soup? No I like chick-en soup! *Clap clap.*

2. Do you like ham and mushroom pie?
No I like tuna pie.

3. Do you like peanut butter rolls?
No I like bacon rolls.

4. Do you like date and walnut cake?
No I like chocolate cake.

5. Do you like caramel ice-cream?
No I like mint ice-cream.

6. Do you like lemonade to drink?
No I like orange squash.

7. Do you like breakfast, lunch or tea?
I don't like one, I like all three!

> When the children are used to the song, divide them into rows, facing each other. One row sings the questions (first three lines) and you choose one child from the other row to sing the answer. The rest of the children in that row must shout or sing 'Me too!' instead of the two claps at the end. Then it is that row's turn to sing the question part of the next verse and so on.

Ann Bryant

**Early years wishing well: Clothes and food**

# What do you like to eat?

## Personal, social and emotional development

★ Give four children four small cards each and ask them to illustrate three cards with food that they like and one with food that they do not like. Laminate the cards and spread them out picture downwards. Invite the children to take turns at picking cards. If a child picks up a picture that they drew of food that they like, they can keep it. If it is one that they do not like, they must say 'No! No! No!' and return it to the table. When they have collected the three food cards that they do like, the children must say 'Yes! Yes! Yes!'. The game finishes when all the children have collected the food cards that they like.

## Communication, language and literacy

★ Make picture and word cards showing all the foods mentioned in the song. Ask the children to sequence the cards so that they tell the story in the song. Mix the cards up again and ask the children which soup, pie and so on they did not like and which they did like. Then invite them to match each picture card with the correct word card.

## Mathematical development

★ Change the role-play area into a baker's shop. Invite the children to make different-shaped and different-sized pies and pasties using play dough. Encourage them to role-play buying and selling the pies using a variety of coins. An adult may need to demonstrate the appropriate behaviour and language to describe the size and shape of the pie required.

## Knowledge and understanding of the world

★ Visit a supermarket to see the different ways that soup can be bought: fresh, powdered and in tins. Buy one flavour of soup in different forms. Take them back to the group and cook them. Let the children taste the different types of soup to see which they like the most.

## Physical development

★ Buy some frozen short crust pastry. Ask the group to help you roll it out to make pies. Show the children how to push the pastry into the pie dish and remove the edges. Use a pie filling of tinned fruit and show the children how to open the tin safely.

## Creative development

★ Put the children in small groups and make up a group story with each child contributing what they like for a particular meal. Start with child 1 saying 'I like to eat… for breakfast', and another child saying 'I like to eat… for lunch' and so on. Record the children to make a story tape for them to listen to.

★ Let the children cut food that they enjoy from magazines and make a group collage of favourite foods.

# Button up!

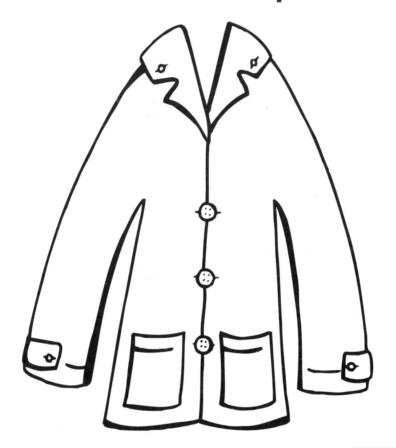

My coat has ○ ○ ○ ○ small buttons. ☐

My coat has  large buttons. ☐

There are  buttons altogether. ☐

# It's a sunny day

# Flower patterns

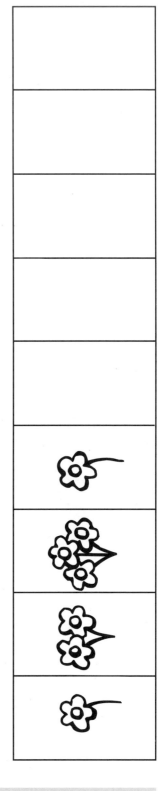

**Early years wishing well: Clothes and food**

# Cake ingredients

## What you need

**Tools**

mixing bowl

tablespoon

electric hand mixer

cake cases

oven glove

apron

bun tin

cooling rack

4 tablespoons

sugar

2 eggs

4 tablespoons

self-raising flour

½ small tub

soft margarine

1 tablespoon

baking powder

# Cake recipe

## What to do

1 Wash hands.

2 Put on apron.

3 Collect ingredients and tools.

4 Put all the ingredients in the bowl.

5 Mix all the ingredients together with the electric mixer (adult only).

6 Put the cake cases in the bun tin.

7 Fill each cake case with 1 tablespoon of mixture.

8 Bake in oven for 10 minutes Gas Mark 4–5 (180–200 °C).

9 Carefully lift out of the oven using the oven glove (adult only).

10 Cool on the cooling rack.

11 Eat for snack!

# What we need

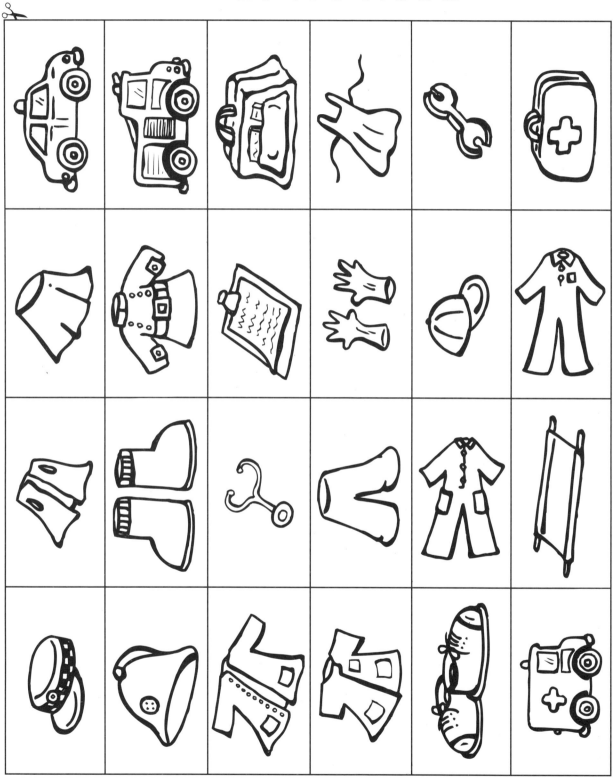

# We wear uniforms

police officer

fire officer

doctor

nurse

car engineer

ambulance driver

# Match them up!

# Puppet play

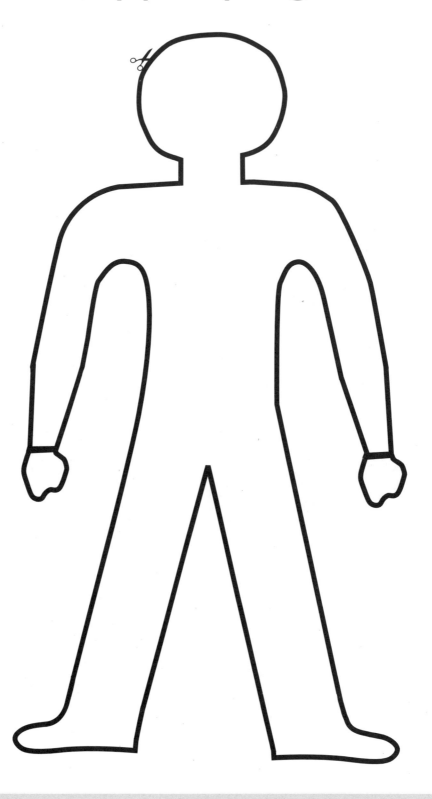

# Dress the doll

# Lunch-box game

**Early years wishing well: Clothes and food**

**■SCHOLASTIC**

# Food spinner

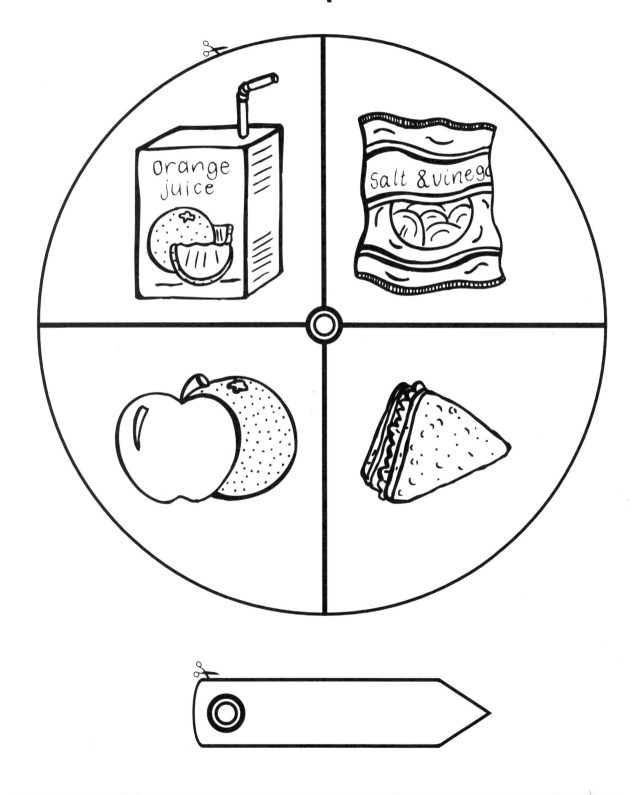

# Let's make salt dough

## Ingredients

2 cups   flour

2 cups   salt

3 drops    oil

## Equipment

1 large mixing bowl

1 stirring spoon

Mix the ingredients together.

# Delicious dishes

# Going shopping

# How many?

# Let's go fishing!

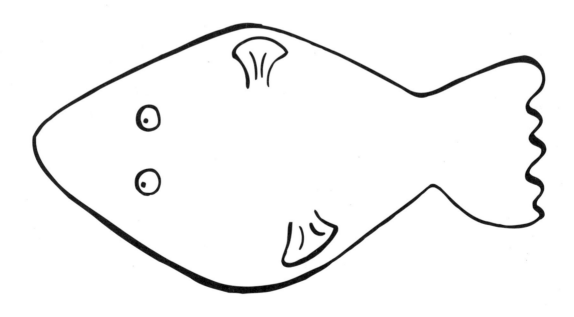

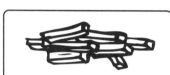

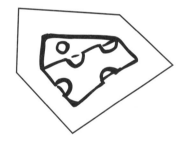

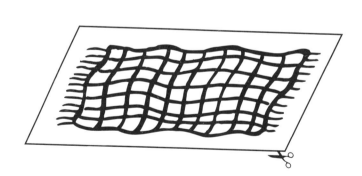

# Picnic time

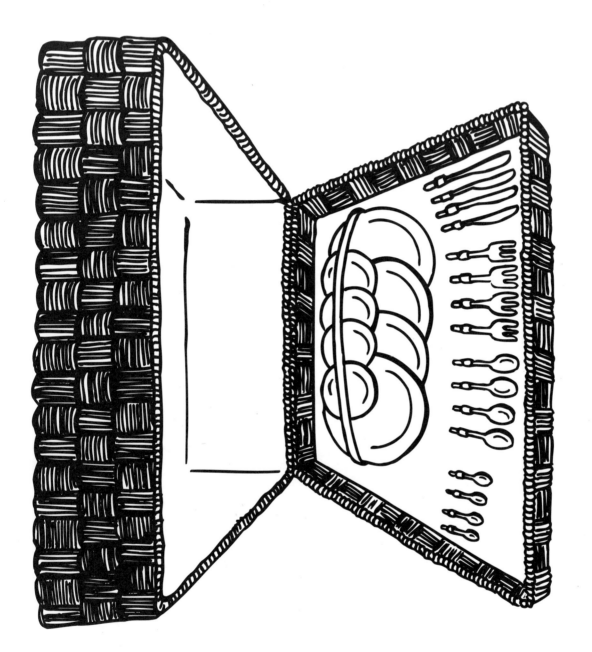

Picnic basket